EDDIE HEMMINGS
COMING OF AGE

EDDIE HEMMINGS COMING OF AGE

A Cricketing Autobiography

EDDIE HEMMINGS
with Graham Otway

STANLEY PAUL
London Sydney Auckland Johannesburg

Stanley Paul & Co. Ltd
An imprint of Random Century Group
20 Vauxhall Bridge Road, London SW1V 2SA

Random Century Australia (Pty) Ltd
20 Alfred Street, Milsons Point, Sydney 2061

Random Century New Zealand Limited
PO Box 40–086, Glenfield, Auckland 10

Century Hutchinson South Africa (Pty) Ltd
PO Box 337, Bergvlei 2012, South Africa

First published 1991

Set in Sabon by Input Typesetting Ltd, London
Printed and bound in Great Britain by Clays Ltd St Ives PLC

A catalogue record for this book is available from the British Library

ISBN 0 09 174867 4

CONTENTS

Acknowledgements

The author and publishers should like to thank AllSport, Patrick Eagar, Ken Kelly and the *Nottingham Evening Post* for the use of their copyright photographs; Roy Ullyett for his *Daily Express* cartoon; and Richard Lockwood (TCCB/Bull Computer Statistics) for Eddie Hemmings' career statistics.

1
LOOKING BACK
Before 1968

There is a somewhat eerie feeling in trying to review a
career in first-class cricket that spans a quarter of
a century. Chewing over a mountain of scrapbooks
religiously kept by my mother that recall many long-forgotten triumphs and failures. Trying to decide with hindsight
whether I took all the right turnings at the various crossroads
in my life.

To all the cricket fans and friends who more recently have
mocked my chubby and unathletic figure while delighting in
my nickname 'The Whale' I offer one immediate response.
At the top of the first page of the very first scrapbook,
Mother has preserved a sixpenny entrance ticket to the
grandly named Mid-Warwickshire Schools Games Association (Primary Schools Athletic Section) Ninth Annual
Sports Day held at Victoria Park, Leamington in July 1956.
Underneath it is a now yellowing extract from the local
newspaper which reveals that Eddie Hemmings of Cashmere
Avenue School finished second in the under-8s 60 yard race.
And just to provide concrete evidence that my first claim to
fame was not a misprint, at the bottom of the page she also
gummed in the certificate which I later received.

Some seven years later early versatility was exhibited when
at the Mid-Warwickshire Second Schools Athletic Association inter-schools meeting of 1963 I received a further
certificate for coming second in the long jump, though in

1

later years, if some wildly inaccurate newspaper reports are to be believed, being in for the high jump became more my speciality.

Those people who followed the career of the late, great cricketer Jim Laker, who turned to journalism and broadcasting after retiring from the game, may recall that in 1981, after I had taken 84 wickets to help Nottinghamshire win the Championship for the first time since 1929, he described me as the best off-spinner available for England. Yet at the start of my career with Warwickshire people classed me as a possible successor at both county and England level to Tom Cartwright, one of the most skilful exponents of medium-pace bowling this country has ever seen.

Then of course there were the scouts from Stoke City who, when I was about to leave school, tempted me with a professional soccer trial at the Victoria Ground. I was tall enough in those days to play centre forward when needed though as years went by other youngsters of the same age seemed to overtake me in the height stakes. I did well enough to be asked back for a second trial but before it could be arranged Warwickshire came in with the offer of a professional contract and I did not pursue a future in soccer any further. I was to go on to play football just below League level in the Midlands for several years, enjoying it thoroughly, and though I might have made the grade and probably a lot more money playing the winter game full-time I never regretted the decision to join the staff at Edgbaston.

Although cricket did not feature highly at my secondary school, enthusiasm for the game existed in the family home as my father, Ted, had been an all-rounder playing for Lockheed in the Warwickshire Works League for years. By the age of ten I was involved in their youth sides and as early as thirteen I was playing with the seniors. I received little formal coaching but my reputation as an attacking middle order batsman and medium-pace bowler quickly spread. As a fourteen-year-old I had very little time for

2

academic studies between playing for the school, Warwickshire Under-15s and the English Schools Cricket Association.
A year later I had progressed to Warwickshire Colts and the
Midland Schools Representative side and even captained
England Schools against the English Public Schools XI in a
youth festival at Southampton. That side contained Chris
Old who was to go on to play for Yorkshire and England,
and George Sharp who later joined Northants giving many
years' service as a wicketkeeper.

Doing the rounds of schoolboy cricket and making steady
progress with my father's wholehearted support was a fairly
carefree existence, but I was quickly brought down to earth
when I moved up a rung and joined the Warwickshire staff
on a full-time basis.

By the standards of the 1960s the set-up at Edgbaston
was a strange mixture of old and new. On the commercial
front the county was light years ahead of its time and there
was no shortage of money. For some years the Warwickshire
Supporters Association had been running a Pool which
raised thousands of pounds every week. The income not
only allowed the ground to develop into one of the country's
top Test centres but was also partially responsible for keeping county cricket alive. In the years following the Second
World War the counties had seen a dramatic slump in
attendances and when I entered the game in 1965 the
resurgence launched by the thrills of the Gillette Cup, which
had started two years previously, was only in its infancy.
There were less amateurs in the game and with rising costs
many less well-managed counties were in serious danger of
going to the wall. Some only owed their continued existence
to the Warwickshire Pool, which was making more money
than was needed at Edgbaston and was able to give out low
interest loans to keep them going. In fact it was only several
years later, when the Test and County Cricket Board was
appointed instead of the MCC to administer the game and
to redistribute the vast income raised from Test matches

fairly among the counties, that many hauled themselves out of debt.

But while Edgbaston thrived financially, dressing room traditions were archaic. In a throwback to the good old amateur days, a dual dressing room system was still in operation when I arrived. There was one for the senior capped players and another for the rest. A couple of years later, when I broke into the first team and began to appear on a semi-regular basis, I hated having to go through the procedure of knocking on the door of the capped players' dressing room and often being told to wait before I could go in and speak to the captain or team-mates with whom I was expected to be an equal on the field of play. There were also other drawbacks.

Although Tom Dollery was the county coach at the time he was very much the sort of person who liked to let youngsters play their cricket naturally. During his career he had himself been a free-flowing batsman and his advice usually consisted of the simple line 'Do what you are best at.' Left very much to my own devices I practised hard and regularly but progress would have been far swifter with more help and there was plenty of experience in the club to draw upon had it been made available to the youngsters. In those days the Warwickshire squad could boast the talents of England captain Mike 'MJK' Smith, wicketkeeper Alan 'AC' Smith and medium-pacers Tom Cartwright and Jack Bannister who had so much experience to pass on. It was frustrating sitting in the uncapped players' dressing rooms during rain breaks or while waiting to bat and not being able to listen to their knowledgeable conversations about the game.

Although no one ever actually came out openly and said it, there was a general principle among the senior pros not actively to help the youngsters because they were guarding their own jobs. If another player learned too much he might one day threaten their place in the side. Given such an austere beginning to my own career it makes me laugh to see youngsters turning up in the 1990s with their sponsored cars and equipment and being spoon-fed by county managers and coaches. If I wanted to learn something new I had to go alone into the net with a bag of balls and experiment for hours on end until I had worked it all out for myself.

Even though I was very much left to chart my own course, once I was on the Warwickshire staff there was no shortage of cricket. During the week I would be playing for either the Colts or the second XI and at weekends I went back to Lockheed and the Coventry Works League where Roly Thompson and I formed a formidable partnership in 1965 occupying the top two places in the bowling averages for most of the summer.

The highlight of that year was travelling with the first team to Derbyshire where I was made twelfth man; the following summer I was given my first-class debut in a friendly against Scotland, taking two victims. I felt in 1967 that I was beginning to make my mark at the club as in all second XI games I took 87 wickets – over 30 more than anyone else – but I was realistic enough to know that Warwickshire had such deep bowling resources that I would still have a long wait before breaking through into the first team. The opportunity finally arrived in early June 1968 when, strangely, I had been going through a rather barren spell. But there can have been few young bowlers over the years who have had quite as dramatic an entry into the County Championship as my debut against Hampshire at Basingstoke.

The vacancy came as Warwickshire suddenly found themselves three players short for a variety of reasons. Bob Barber, our opening batsman and leg spinner, had made himself unavailable because he was trying to combine a business career with cricket and on this occasion the former took priority. David Brown had been called up by England to face the Australians in the second Test at Lord's and Tom Cartwright had an injury. Even then I was not considered next in the queue and the morning before the match was in the nets at Edgbaston with the other members of the second XI squad when I was summoned to the secretary's office and told to make my way down to Hampshire immediately. Apparently David Cook, who had originally been chosen to take one of the places, had also been found to be unavailable.

The early omens for the day that lay ahead were not very bright: Hampshire's varied pace attack made up of Test players Derek Shackleton and Bob Cottam, along with Butch White who had been selected for an overseas tour, went through our batting pretty quickly and going in at number eight I was fourth highest scorer with 18 before being bowled by White and we were all out well before tea.

Against Jack Bannister and Bill Blenkiron the two Barrys, Richards and Reed, made a steady start to Hampshire's reply and they had already posted 27 on the board when skipper AC Smith decided it was time for me to bowl. Again there was little hint of the drama to follow as I suffered a slight attack of first-night nerves. One early delivery actually bounced not far from my feet after I accidentally hit the top of the stumps while bringing my arm over. The ball stopped dead halfway down the pitch and Reed stepped down and used a 'free hit' to pick up a single.

But all the embarrassment was long forgotten the next morning as I opened a series of telegrams from friends and members of the family and checked in the newspaper that I hadn't dreamed up the following scoreboard.

My luck changed beyond all recognition with the first ball after tea when Barry Reed edged an away-swinger into the hands of Rohan Khanhai at first slip; seven balls later Richard Lewis drove a sharp chance to cover and then came the most satisfying wicket of them all.

Hampshire's Roy Marshall, a white Barbadian, had played Test cricket for the West Indies and was widely recognised at the time as one of the hardest strikers of the ball in the game. But I got him first ball with a brute: it

Warwickshire 145

Hampshire first innings:

B A Richards not out	64
B L Reed c Khanhai b Hemmings	16
R V Lewis c Gibbs b Hemmings	2
R E Marshall b Hemmings	0
P J Sainsbury c Khanhai b Hemmings	14
D A Livingstone lbw b Hemmings	0
R M C Gilliatt lbw b Hemmings................................	2
B S V Timms not out..	14
Extras (b2, lb2)	4
Total (6 wkts 47 overs)	116

Fall of wickets: 1/36 2/40 3/40 4/84 5/84 6/89
Bowling: Bannister 14–6–19–0 Blenkiron 5–0–19–0 Hemmings 18–3–51–6 Gibbs 10–1–23–0

swung away from him in the air then cut back into him off the seam, nipping through the gap between bat and pad to rip out the middle stump. I had taken three wickets in nine balls and at one stage, later, as Hampshire were reduced to 86 for 6 I actually had figures of 6 for 36.

By then it had occurred to me that I might yet take all ten wickets on my first appearance in the Championship, but two things put an abrupt stop to such wild thoughts. The first was Barry Richards, the great South African who had turned down a chance to play for Lancashire and in his first season with Hampshire had already made a major impact by scoring a century in each innings in only his third game at Northampton. I was later to enjoy many a tussle with Richards who was one of the finest players of spin bowling I have ever faced, having a technique which gave him so much extra time to play the ball.

While I had been running through the Hampshire middle order Richards was quietly accumulating, but when he had made 38 he tried to swing me away on the leg side and got a top edge. The ball looped gently to John Jamieson at deep point and while it presented a straightforward catch, Jamieson let it go straight through his hands and it bounced off his ample chest and ended up on the ground.

The other factor which halted my progress was the heavy rain which fell in Basingstoke overnight. Although AC Smith threw the ball straight to me when play resumed on the second day after a fifteen minute delay, the pendulum had swung. Richards, at his fluent best, took 21 runs off my first two overs and with the ball quickly beginning to resemble a wet sponge after it was hammered all over a wet outfield, I could not get it to swing as I had done on the previous afternoon. Richards went on to make 133 and we lost the match by six wickets. While I scored 11 in our second innings I didn't get another bowl as Hampshire easily scored 60 in their second innings for victory. Still, at least my mother had a fistful of new cuttings – this time from the national newspapers – to glue into the scrapbooks.

2
MAKING THE GRADE
1969–78

Despite my explosive entry into county cricket, it was to be several years before I could lay claims to being a regular in the Warwickshire side and a few more before I could call myself established. Between the ages of 20 and 25 are probably the hardest years for any professional cricketer. The pay for youngsters in county cricket is negligible and unless they are exceedingly gifted deep supplies of patience are necessary as they try to progress.

Money was certainly tight in the Hemmings household in those formative years. After Chris and I married in 1971 and bought our first home in Leamington it was only the fact that for several years she had a good job as personal assistant to the chairman of a local firm that kept us going; my contribution from the wages at Warwickshire was negligible.

A lot of it went on running a reliable car which I needed to get me to the ground and back each day, a round trip of 50 miles. When we paid out £1,000 for a new Mini it stretched us to the limit but even though I could only just get my 'coffin' with all my kit in it on to the back seat it was all we could afford. We couldn't afford to go out too often socially, though when Mike Smith, the Warwickshire captain, bought Wootton Court, a small hotel and country club, a small group of us regularly met there for a drink on Saturday nights.

I was prepared to put up with the hardship because I was desperately keen to succeed in the game and I set my sights high. I wanted to play for England. But I sometimes wonder just how many would-be world-class cricketers have been lost to cricket in England because of the poor starting wages. Until recent years in Australia State cricket was always a part-time profession to be combined with a career outside of the game, but with just a basic job at a county, players are meant to be available full-time between April and September with no time, or for that matter energy, left to hold down some other sort of job as well. Teenagers straight out of school are often put off cricket as a career when they know they could earn ten times the money on building sites and those students who have gone on to university take some convincing to turn their backs on lucrative jobs in the traditional professions and commerce. Although things have improved markedly with the Professional Cricketers' Association negotiating minimum rates it still makes cricket almost a vocation for those players who do not reach Test stature where big money is now available.

Having chosen my lot when I first signed for Warwickshire and been in and out of the first team, as the '60s turned into the '70s there came a time when I had to examine my progress closely and weigh up the best course for my career to follow. I had been recognised from the start as an all-rounder but even though I could take wickets and score a few valuable runs, the fact that my game was made up of bits and pieces meant I was never really challenging for a permanent place in the side, merely filling gaps. In the batting department Warwickshire were packed out with class players like Mike Smith, Rohan Khanhai, John Jamieson and Dennis Amiss. Given that I was batting well down the order at seven, eight and nine, my opportunities were severely restricted. The bowling was spearheaded by players like Tom Cartwright, David Brown and Jack Bannister who had so much experience that I knew it was going to be impossible to dislodge them. And when I did play alongside them I didn't get the opportunities to bowl when the ball was new and at its hardest.

The first decision to let my batting slip and concentrate on bowling was based on the simplest of logic. It doesn't take a genius to realise that when a batsman is at the crease it only takes one mistake for him to lose his wicket, whereas a bowler has a great advantage with the ball in his hand six times an over. He can bowl one bad ball and still have a chance of redeeming himself with any of the other five. But as a bowler I didn't have the extra yards of pace to beat batsmen on the sort of dead flat wickets that were the norm at Edgbaston. In between second XI games I would go back to play for Dad's old Lockheed side at the weekends and regularly run through sides, but it was a completely different world from the county side where most of the opposition teams had at least one batsman who had played Test cricket and maybe a couple of others who were put in the promising category.

So as our strong first team was tying for the Championship in 1971 and winning the pennant a year later, I began to look the other way, knowing that when Lance Gibbs eventually retired the county would be looking for a slow bowler. I deliberately use the word 'slow' rather than 'spin' because in fact the change in my bowling would purely require a change of pace. From my early days in cricket I could always swing the ball when the conditions were right, but day in and day out I was basically a medium-pace stock bowler of cutters – balls which moved off the seam. And since with the grip that I employed my cutters were basically fast off-spinners, the transformation was not that difficult. Of course a slow bowler needs a great deal of accuracy which comes with practice, confidence and experience, but all I had to do was dramatically cut down my pace and run up. Once that had been worked out I then had to learn the variations in flight and speed which spinners employ to out-think batsmen.

The transition period took its toll on my first team opportunities and one or two odd names appear in the bowling averages from the *Wisdens* of those years which tell the story. For instance, while many people remember AC Smith as a Warwickshire batsman, wicketkeeper and captain, in 1972 when I spent the whole of the summer in the second XI he bowled more than 200 overs, topping the county averages with 20 wickets at an average of 22.45. Generally he bowled medium pace in-swing and on rain-affected wickets he could get the leg cutter going and prove pretty effective. He was not a more penetrative bowler than me and did roughly the same job, but he was captain at the time and therefore in the side, whereas I, like any other youngster, always had to earn a place on merit.

Of all the captains I played under at Warwickshire, and even later at Notts, AC got my vote as the best. When he was behind the wicket he seemed to know instinctively when it was the right time for me to bowl; he seemed to be able to tell just by the way the ball went into his gloves what sort of form I was in and he was rarely wrong.

The following year my opportunities began to increase but 1974 was the first time when I began to be considered a regular in the side, having completed the transition in my game. Handled well by AC throughout the summer I bowled more than 600 overs, picking up 82 wickets. And in July, when Lancashire came to Edgbaston, I earned myself a very welcome pay rise as well as the right to use the senior players' dressing room. We asked them to score 214 to win in three hours and I put that target totally beyond their reach in a mean ten-over spell that cost only 15 runs but, more importantly, contained four wickets – three victims being Barry Wood, Frank Hayes and Clive Lloyd who were all Test players. Our attempts to win the game were resisted by a stubborn last-wicket stand between Peter Lever and

Jack Simmons but I finished with career-best figures of 7–57 and after the game it was announced that I had been awarded my county cap, receiving the relevant salary increase.

I disown any association with the coincidence that my arrival as a first team regular was the start of a steady decline in Warwickshire's fortunes from the title challengers of the early '70s to one of the Championship's weaker sides.

The problems at Edgbaston could never be blamed on a lack of experience or talent, or even money to attract good players: all three elements were available in abundance. But by 1975 we had slipped to fourteenth, our lowest placing since 1960, and there were no acceptable excuses as at one stage, from the end of July, we went fourteen matches without a victory in either the Championship or one-day cricket. In the members' bar accusing fingers were pointing in every direction, but there was so much wrong that the blame could not be placed firmly in any spot.

A change of captaincy during the winter did not help as AC Smith retired, and with David Brown taking his place I felt the effects more keenly than most of the other players on the staff. In the summer of 1975 I bowled 799 overs at less than three runs apiece which was quite an achievement on the Edgbaston wickets, but the fact that I took only 58 wickets proved that, while I was being bowled to exhaustion, it was not always at a time when I could have inflicted most damage on the opposition.

Brown bravely tried to make up for his tactical short-comings by bowling more than 640 overs himself that summer, hoping that his enthusiastic approach to the game would rub off on others. It was claimed that the absence of our other England fast bowler Bob Willis for most of the summer had also left us short in the new ball department, but I beg to disagree.

Willis had returned home early from Australia the previous winter for medical treatment on a knee injury. At first it seemed to have done the trick as he bowled well in one Benson and Hedges Cup game against Worcestershire but a few days later he entered hospital to have a cartilage removed from his right knee and inflamed tissue from under both his knee-caps. He returned to action late in August, picking up thirteen wickets in three Championship games, and that suggested to onlookers that his absence had been a key factor, but it wasn't. For all his success as a magnificent fast bowler in Test matches Willis was not a contributor at county level. He tended to 'lord it' a bit around the dressing room, letting everyone know exactly who he was and it was not good for team morale to see him trying his heart out in Tests yet barely going through the motions with the county side. He played few games for us over the years but always seemed to be fit and raring to go whenever the England selectors sent for him.

Another cause of irritation in the dressing room was the number of overseas players we had on the books – five played for the first team that summer – Rohan Khanhai, Alvin Kallicharran, Deryck Murray, Bill Bourne and Earl Harris. It took Lord's many years to realise the harm done to the development of home-bred players by the mass of imports from overseas, but I and several other Warwickshire players felt sometimes that we were playing for the West Indies second XI at Edgbaston. Those of us who were born in the county often struggled for a place but the red carpet just seemed to be rolled out for players born in the Caribbean. It was even more annoying that, while money could always be found to pay the imports their high wages, the county always pleaded poverty whenever we went in to discuss new contracts.

If there was one playing reason behind our decline it was the potential strength of our batting. With four recognised Test batsmen in Kallicharran, Khanhai, Amiss and Jamieson, at the head of our order, few opposition captains were prepared to declare and set us reasonable fourth-innings targets.

In the winter of 1976–77 I had a small shock on the medical front. I suddenly found myself short of breath and panting heavily whenever I exerted myself, particularly if I went on training. There were no problems when I was sitting quietly but after a time I took the matter to my doctor. He was puzzled at first and referred me to a specialist but it was only when I went back to the doctor that he cracked the symptoms and announced that I had asthma. Since I had suffered from eczema all my life and the two conditions are thought to be linked it should not have come as a great surprise. Fortunately it meant no great change to my life or threat to my cricketing career. In any event, after having eczema for many years, coping with asthma proved to be almost a doddle.

Since that day, however, I have had to carry a Ventolin inhaler with me at all times which brings almost instant relief. Some people would be surprised how many sportsmen actually suffer from the condition with no effect on their performance – Ian Botham is one cricketer who immediately springs to mind – and in all the years since it was diagnosed I can remember only two occasions when an asthma attack has been bad enough to force me to leave the cricket field for medication. Even then I was back on the field after ten to fifteen minutes.

There was nothing to suggest at the start of 1978 that it would be my last season at Warwickshire. I was an established capped player in a side that was trying to rebuild after losing the services of Mike Smith, John Jamieson and Rohan Khanhai at the end of the previous season and did not feel under any threat, although the county had given a contract to Chris Clifford. He had played at the start of the 1970s for Yorkshire and came with a strong recommendation from Geoff Boycott. Since giving up the game full-time, Clifford had taken to school teaching and would only be available to us during the school holidays. He was obviously not a long term bet and I was therefore surprised and hurt to find myself relegated to the second XI from the moment he arrived in mid July.

I was to stay there brooding for the rest of the season, giving my all to the team and trying to help the youngsters but knowing I should have been with the firsts. It was during that period that a storm broke at Edgbaston over the decision by Dennis Amiss to join up with Kerry Packer's rebel cricket tour in Australia. While it shouldn't have had any effect on my own plight at the time I found myself caught up in a dressing-room controversy. From all over the cricketing establishment there were howls of outrage at the Packer organisation and dire warnings of the possible consequences for county cricketers.

At Warwickshire feelings ran strongly against Amiss. A court case the previous winter which the Packer side had won prevented the Test and County Cricket Board from banning from the Championship players who had been involved in the circus but Amiss returned from Australia to find open hostility in the Warwickshire dressing room. To his great credit Amiss refused to let the bitterness affect his cricket and he had a magnificent summer scoring 2,001 runs in the Championship at an average of 55. But whatever he did on the field was not enough to stop the players holding a series of meetings and even some supporters getting together to demand his head. Since I was in the second XI when matters began to reach a climax I was not involved, until our new skipper John Whitehouse wrote to the committee on behalf of 'all' the capped players condemning Amiss for joining the Packer organisation. I knew nothing of the letter until I read about it in the press. Since I was a capped player I was furious that the captain had signed a protest in my name without even consulting me and I demanded and got a public apology. The fact was that I did not blame Amiss at all for joining up with Packer. Cricketers had

16

always been poorly paid at county level and even playing fees for England before Packer stepped in Test matches were only £250 a time – a pittance compared with the money earned by top stars in other sports.

In some ways I could understand the worries of the 'bread and butter' professionals who saw their careers threatened if international cricket was going to be split into two camps with a subsequent cut in Test match income, but in the event all forecasts of benefits to the game predicted by members of the Packer camp turned out to be true. For years cricket administrators had in many cases been living in the dark ages – amateurs trying to run a professional sport on a hand-to-mouth basis. Yet the lessons learned from Packer about marketing and television fees changed many attitudes in this country. Test match fees suddenly shot up to over £1,000 a time which was an added incentive for promising youngsters to stay in the game and try to reach the top instead of seeking their fortunes in industry. And the extra money that began to flow into English cricket through the introduction of Test match sponsorship by Cornhill Insurance filtered right down through the game, improving the lot of those of us playing at ground level.

By taking my stand against the captain and other senior players in the dressing room I was not entirely popular; nevertheless the treatment which finally made me leave the county was shoddy. At the end of the summer, spent playing in the second XI because of Clifford's presence in the firsts, Warwickshire offered me just another one year contract, when all the other players on the staff (with the exception of Dennis Amiss who was mulling over the possibility of retirement) had been offered two years.

I regarded it as being given a year's notice either to find another county or to quit the first-class game. Warwickshire had told me in as many words that I had to play brilliantly the following summer to be given a contract for 1980. After fourteen years with the county it was desperately disappointing to have to start all over again and prove myself in the space of four months. I felt I had done enough over the years to demonstrate my ability. I firmly believe I had been made a scapegoat for Warwickshire's lack of success and decided to make the break. If I couldn't find another county I was going to give up first-class cricket and find a new job in the world outside.

The only person who counted at Edgbaston who seemed to appreciate my services was our coach Alan Oakman. After I had averaged 26 with the bat and taken 47 wickets at an average of 13.12 in only eleven games he wrote:

> 'Dear Eddie,
> Just a brief note to thank you very much for your help during the second half of the season. I know you must have been very disappointed being left out of the first XI but at that particular time I think you would agree that you had not been bowling particularly well. However, I would say that I was most impressed with your attitude in the second XI and also with the encouragement you gave to people, such as Gordon Lord.'

The post at the end of the season also included a letter from Edgar Hiley who was then Chairman of the Warwickshire Supporters Association. He wrote:

> 'Dear Eddie,
> My Committee was sorry to learn that you are leaving Warwickshire and they have asked me to extend their very best wishes to you for a happy and successful career with Notts. Over the years you have given us all much enjoyment and it is our wish that you should accept the enclosed gift from the Association as a token of the regard in which you are held and a "thank you" for the pleasure that you have given us on so many occasions.'

The 'enclosed gift' turned out to be a cheque for £2,000 which came as a great surprise. Considering that Warwickshire had only offered me £4,500 to play on for one season, it represented a great deal of money to us and it arrived at

18

a time when I was out of work and had not at that stage been approached about a move to Nottinghamshire.

In fact I had virtually resigned myself to finding a job and playing out the rest of my career in the Leagues. There was money to be made there at the weekends but I hadn't really got a clue what sort of a job I was going to do for the rest of the week. Cricket had been my life since leaving school and since I was still some months short of my thirtieth birthday and hadn't foreseen my full-time playing days coming to such an abrupt end, I had not made any contingency plans.

It was towards the end of September, as I was mooching around the house fairly depressed with things in general, that the phone call came which was to change my life. Chris answered and when she said that Ken Taylor wanted to talk to me my immediate response was 'Who?' It turned out that the Nottinghamshire manager had asked Warwickshire for permission to approach me. As I sat on the floor in the dining room he spent half an hour convincing me that I should drive up the M1 and sign on at Trent Bridge. 'Oh yes,' I thought, 'I have heard that one before.' But I did drive to Trent Bridge to find out what Notts had to offer and it was just like going to see my auntie, who actually lived in the city – so friendly it was almost untrue, the complete opposite of the austere organisation that I had played under for twelve years at Edgbaston.

I found the Notts chairman, John Heatley, in the bar. I am sure he wouldn't mind me saying that it was to be a fairly regular meeting place for us from then on. After speaking to him and having a chat with Ken Taylor I was sold on the idea of signing up with them. It was to be a decision that changed everything in my life.

3

A COUNTY WITH AMBITION
1978–81

The forward-looking approach and friendliness of the officials at Trent Bridge and the need to get myself another job in cricket quickly to keep my career going prompted me to take up their offer with barely a second thought, though the £4,000 a year salary was actually £500 less than I had been offered at Edgbaston. But I arrived in the East Midlands at a time when the county was going through a period of transition.

There had been no trophies won by the club since the County Championship of 1929 and just six months earlier there had been ructions over the captaincy. Notts had intended that Clive Rice would lead the side in 1978 but with the season barely a week away it was announced that he had signed with Kerry Packer. The committee had little alternative but to take the job away from Rice since earlier they, themselves, had written to Sussex demanding they sack Tony Greig for his part in the Packer affair. Mike Smedley, who had been leading the side since 1975, had agreed to take the captaincy on again, though with no dramatic improvement in fortunes, and he was still in charge when I reported for my first spell of pre-season training in 1979.

The signing of both myself and Mike Bore from Yorkshire during the winter had given Notts an experienced spin attack to back up the international pace-bowling department of Rice and Richard Hadlee. With their batting as well as Derek

Randall, who at the time was probably at his peak as an England batsman, in the middle order it was no wonder that Ken Taylor, who was beginning his first season as manager, was expecting great things from us.

After so much frustration in the Warwickshire second XI at the end of the previous season I was as keen as mustard. I picked up a few early Benson and Hedges wickets, with three in one game against Yorkshire, and turned in several useful Championship performances without actually bowling the side to victory in the first few months. I was also contributing runs, making 85 not out against Hampshire at Bournemouth early in June, and was averaging around 30 at the end of the month when we lay second in the table. Admittedly we were already 69 points behind Essex who had got off to a flying start, while our progress had been hampered by having three early matches abandoned without a ball being bowled.

I had found it very easy to slip into the Trent Bridge set-up where we all changed in one room instead of the separate facilities for seniors and juniors that had made Edgbaston a divided camp. On paper we batted down to ten and with two all-rounders we could field six bowlers in most games. But while I kept my head down, anxious to impress as one of the new boys, and got on with my job, life was not too peaceful in the committee room.

Despite our healthy position in the table Taylor had become convinced that Smedley was not the right man to lead the side and he had plenty of supporters within the club. Smedley had spent fifteen years at Trent Bridge and was greatly admired as a valuable servant and reliable batsman, but as captain he was very down to earth, a dour leader with few ideas. Taylor wanted someone much more dynamic to give the side flair and so just after we had recorded our fourth win of the season against Gloucestershire at Trent Bridge in mid July – a game to which Rice contributed 129 and a haul of 5–44 in their first innings –

Smedley was sacked and Rice, despite the events of fifteen months earlier, took control.

Sadly Smedley, bitter at his treatment, left the club soon after, but we immediately responded by walloping Yorkshire by eight wickets at Worksop, even though Geoff Boycott spent six hours trying to keep us out single-handed by scoring 170 in their second innings. Unfortunately for him, wickets kept tumbling at the other end and the three I picked up helped us towards the win.

That game was probably our highest point in my first season which was to taper off quite dramatically in the last couple of months. Having won four out of thirteen games under Smedley we achieved only one more victory in eight matches under Rice and slipped down to finish ninth in the table. And while we had high hopes in the Gillette Cup, these came to a halt when Sussex beat us in a low-scoring quarter-final at Hove. The change of captaincy had certainly brought about a change in attitude at the club; Rice was harsh and ruthless but at times in those final few weeks his inexperience as captain showed through.

It was a hard first season for me but not entirely unsatisfactory. The family had not moved over from Leamington and while I stayed with my aunt in Nottingham who treated me with all the kindness in the world I could only snatch brief nights back at home with the family – a position I was determined to rectify in the close season.

The one return trip to Warwickshire that summer which did give me immense pleasure was our Championship game against my old team-mates at Edgbaston. My bowling was not too flattered in their first innings as I could only manage 2–83, while centuries from Dennis Amiss and Andy Lloyd in a partnership of 214 allowed them to make 327–4 from their 100 overs. We managed to get within seven runs of that total but then the wicket began to wear and Bore and I ran through their second innings to set us up for a seven-wicket victory. Having spent thirteen years, the last few certainly in an unhappy state, at Warwickshire, it was some revenge for my treatment as I picked up 5–74, and it certainly brought a lively reaction from the crowd. There were some boos but there were also many cheers from old friends who thought the county had made the wrong decision in letting me go.

I had played in all our first-class fixtures in that first season, bowling 692 overs and taking 57 wickets at 29.50 runs apiece, and in early September was honoured to receive an engraved tankard from the Notts sponsors Home Brewery as the county's bowling award. With Bore having bowled many of his 669 overs from the other end it was the start of a spinning partnership that I would like to think played an important part in Notts' success in the years that followed.

I think any spinner would admit that it is always helpful having a slow bowling partner and Bore and I were to grow to understand each other's moods. He would know when to bowl defensively if it was my day and I was taking wickets at the other end, and I would often do likewise for him to keep the pressure on when he was getting among the batsmen.

It is a pity that too many people outside of the Notts dressing room have only one memory of Bore's contribution at Notts and that was the dramatic finish to the 1984 season when we travelled to Taunton for the last game of the season knowing that a 24-point victory would give us the title. It turned out to be a thrilling game for which much credit must go to Ian Botham, who was leading Somerset at the time.

After rain had taken three hours out of the first day of the match, Rice had kept it open by declaring our first innings 52 runs adrift of the opposition. That put the onus on Botham to set us some sort of target but he was in a Catch-22 situation. If the target was too easy and we waltzed to victory there would be an outcry from Essex who were chasing us for the title. On the other hand, if he kept the

Somerset second innings going too long he would doubtless have received an icy blast in Afrikaans from Rice. As it turned out, Botham got it exactly right by setting us a Gillette Cup-style target of 297 in 60 overs and when, after Rice had hammered 98 off only 109 balls with three sixes, we were beginning to falter, Botham made sure our chances did not die an early death by keeping his spinners in action right to the last.

Bore's reputation as a batsman was hardly one to be feared but having seen many of the players higher up the order get themselves out somewhat recklessly, he launched a last-ditch push to try to secure the Championship for us. Thirty-six runs had been wanted off the last three overs and when young slow-left-arm spinner Stephen Booth ran up to bowl the final six balls of the season, fourteen were needed with Bore facing and our last man Andy Pick at the non-striker's end. Bore had scored ten of them before, from the fifth ball of the over, he launched Booth in the direction of the long off boundary where the Somerset substitute Richard Ollis took a well-judged catch.

We were heartbroken to lose out on the title at the last gasp. Had the ball landed a couple of feet short of him the batsman would have got two and the final ball would have been the decider. Had it gone a few feet either side of Ollis it would have been the winning hit. There was no consoling Bore at the end of the game but he deserved only praise for a brave innings which almost pulled off a remarkable win. In any event he had almost succeeded where his batting peers – myself included, since I was out stumped with only one to my name – had failed. Victory at Taunton would have given me my second Championship Winners' Medal in three seasons since, after the hectic events of my first season at Trent Bridge, Ken Taylor's ambitions of building a Championship-winning side had soon become a reality.

We showed a dramatic improvement in 1980, finishing third in the Championship race. This was the club's highest position since the title had been won in 1929, though some distance behind the London clubs Middlesex and Surrey. I started slowly and was left out of the first team for several Benson games but then came back to play a major part in a victory over Glamorgan, contributed significantly in a win against Surrey and almost spun Notts to another success at Leicestershire.

Many of our early problems, especially away from home, stemmed from the opposition preparing flat wickets to try to counter our attack which was beginning to acquire a fearsome reputation, but as we began to climb up the table the Notts committee rewarded both me and Bore with our county caps. I had been through the ceremony with Warwickshire but it certainly had a lot more significance for Bore whose efforts had never been recognised in the same way by Yorkshire – though when Rice went to present him with his Notts cap at Leicester no one could find him since he had sloped off to the physio's room to have treatment on an injured finger!

A season which promised so much ended, however, without a trophy again. Although we were in the Championship prize money we went out to the eventual winners early on in both the Benson and Hedges and Gillette Cups and spent much of the time anchored at the foot of the John Player League. Our main shortcoming was the fact that we went into many matches with our seam attack weakened by injuries. Hadlee, exhausted by a winter of action in New Zealand, was troubled by the strain of playing cricket all year round and played in only seven games all summer. Rice, too, had his share of problems and the back-up bowlers were also struggling.

Bore's finger injury kept him out of the side for a spell and the result was that my 564 overs in the summer were nearly 200 more than those bowled by any other individual. I was pleased to finish 19th in the national averages and among my 77 wickets were three taken in late August against the Australians when they arrived at Trent Bridge for their final match in preparation for the Centenary Test at Lord's.

We dealt their confidence a severe blow in winning by an innings and 76 runs which was the highest margin of victory over the tourists by an English county since 1888. The win attracted a great deal of publicity for us in the press and for the first time my name was mentioned as a possible future England player – though that honour was still to be a couple of years away.

During the winter of 1980–81 the Test and County Cricket Board abolished the restriction of 100 overs per first innings in Championship matches, in a move which it was claimed would encourage the use of spin bowling. For nearly a decade counties had been placing less emphasis on spin, especially in one-day games, and it was beginning to be reflected in a weakness in that department at Test level. But while making a move to help us with one hand they somehow managed to deal us a counter-blow with the other by making a new ball available to bowling sides after 85 overs and I felt if anything it was going to cut down my workload in 1981.

At the start of the season I was fit for anything, however, having been persuaded by our young seam bowler Kevin Cooper to return to soccer after a three-year winter break. We both turned out for Apsley Old Boys Reserves in the Notts Central Alliance League every Saturday, with me playing striker and him in the defence, though he was the only centre half I'd ever known who couldn't head the ball.

While I was getting frozen on the local soccer pitches the county were involved in lengthy discussions with Hadlee and eventually he agreed to return to the county for another year despite his reservations on the toll that playing cricket seven days a week would take on his fitness. He came back bowling off an experimental shorter run that was to become his hallmark over the next seven years and help us to a succession of trophies.

With Hadlee fit and raring to go and the revised ruling over the availability of new balls I could probably have got long odds from the local bookies on the chances of me ending up our leading wicket-taker for the second season running. But from the very first game when we travelled down to Canterbury to play Kent, I hardly seemed to be out of the headlines. We were desperately unlucky not to open the new campaign with a victory after asking the home side to score 242 to win in 195 minutes. After taking two wickets in their first innings I followed up with 6–80 as they lost wickets regularly in the run chase and we were only to be denied a win at the death by a defiant last-wicket stand between Kevin Jarvis and Derek Underwood.

It was the seamers who opened our winning account with an eight-wicket victory in the East Midlands Derby against Leicestershire, but when Gloucestershire were among the early season visitors to Trent Bridge I had a field day in their second innings, taking 6–21 in only 12 overs as we moved to the top of the Championship table. The return also put me top of the national bowling averages for the first time in my life and there was no sign of the Notts bandwagon slowing down. Nor was my strike rate diminishing as I had another six wickets as a result of our drawn game with Yorkshire at Bradford and five against Middlesex, though our defeat against one of the strongest sides in the country left us all fuming.

On a turning wicket we didn't bat terribly well in our second innings, but still had an outside chance of a draw when I top-edged a ball from John Emburey into my face. That happened dead on 5pm and after I had had treatment for five minutes I decided I had to leave the field. Although Emburey and Phil Edmonds were turning the ball at right angles, Kevin Cooper fought on for another fifteen overs. But when Bore was our ninth man out I went back to the wicket with what I thought was only another five overs to be bowled.

With the Middlesex field packed around the bat, Cooper and I felt we had done enough to prevent our big rivals from taking the points by staying together until 6pm. But just when we thought the game should have finished – and Middlesex had bowled 20 overs since the injury – umpires Don Oslear and Derek Shackleton directed that the last hour had only begun after my treatment had ended at 5.05pm and ordered that two more overs should be bowled. Sadly Cooper fell to a catch by Clive Radley off the seventh extra ball and we were beaten by 112 runs. Our players and the crowd were incensed, especially since Law 17 stated that if there was an interruption at the start of the last hour the minimum number of overs to be bowled should be reduced. We all knew that those extra 16 points that Middlesex had picked up could be vital if, as expected, they were up near the top of the table at the end of the season.

The committee took the matter to the Test and County Cricket Board who then in my opinion made the strangest of decisions. They agreed with us that the umpires should have called a halt to the match after the 20 overs had been bowled and were then wrong not to inform the crowd or the ground authority of their decision to let play continue. But having reached the conclusion that technically Middlesex should not have received the extra overs the Board decided the result should stand.

It was to be a fortnight before we returned to winning ways with a home victory over Worcestershire but we quickly consolidated our position as title contenders with a win against Lancashire and after a reverse at Leicester began a tremendous run at the start of August, rolling over Surrey at Trent Bridge by an innings and 15 runs.

For a month my own form had been rather subdued but all that changed as we went to New Road to take on Worcestershire. On a drying wicket Clive Rice decided I should be given the new ball in both innings with Hadlee and I had the rare distinction of bowling unchanged throughout the game. On my way to match figures of 10 for 130 I passed 200 wickets for Notts in only my third season at the club and I might have had one more had it not been for another bizarre clash with the rulebook. On this occasion Phil Neale played a stroke which rebounded off the helmet of Basher Hassan fielding at short-leg into Hadlee's hands, but the umpires ruled it an unfair catch. I suppose there was some compensation later when Tim Curtis, in trying to prevent a delivery spinning back onto his stumps, hit his wicket.

That performance against Worcestershire took my tally of wickets for the season to 61 and brought me my first hint of England recognition. With the fifth Ashes Test of the summer due to be played a couple of days later at Edgbaston, John Emburey had reported for the match with a slight injury and the selectors asked Nottingham to place me on standby.

Emburey recovered in time, however, and I was left to prepare for our next match with second-in-the-table Sussex. It was billed as a battle for the title but turned out be an exciting draw that decided nothing. It was not played on the best of Trent Bridge wickets as Sussex spinner Chris Waller bowled us out cheaply. I responded with 9–151 in both their innings and the close of the final day saw Bore and me in desperate straits trying to hold out for four overs against Imran Khan and Garth Le Roux in full flight to secure a draw.

For the second game running against Sussex Rice had not hesitated to throw me the new ball at the start of an innings and it was becoming clear that his leadership, if slightly unorthodox at times, could provide the occasional extra spark that might make all the difference in the end.

We had our work cut out initially, however, as we moved on to Edgbaston when Dennis Amiss and Geoff Humpage helped them amass 331 for nine declared. We also called a halt to our innings early once a century from Derek Randall made sure we had all four batting bonus points in the bag, but a close match was suddenly swung in our direction by Hadlee, whose nine-over second-innings burst produced three wickets for six runs and they crashed to 49 all out, and by taking the extra half hour we secured victory inside two days.

Hadlee was also in rampant form as we moved on to Cleethorpes for the traditional August Bank Holiday fixture against Northants, producing eight wickets as we won by an innings and 53 runs. We returned home to Trent Bridge for the final two games of the season top of the table, knowing that two wins would end the county's long quest for glory.

We knew that our nearest neighbours and fiercest rivals Derbyshire were unlikely to be generous in our penultimate game, but if I felt that the England selectors needed any more coaxing to include me in their winter tour plans for India and Sri Lanka I could not have provided them with a better advertisement for my skills. Brian Close, one of the Test selectors, had been at our losing Gillette Cup semi-final with Derbyshire and had asked me quietly whether I would be available to go on the tour and my hopes were high.

Continuing a remarkable sequence of winning the toss, Rice asked Derbyshire to bat and although Barry Wood and Budd Hill put on 55 for the first wicket, I found plenty of encouraging turn and bounce once the ball was tossed in my direction, taking seven of their last eight wickets to fall while 69 runs were scored. On a pitch that certainly wasn't easy our batsmen struggled as well but with John Birch scoring 62 not out we gained a useful 57-run first-innings lead. When they batted second time around the Derbyshire side seemed more intent on survival than taking the game to the bowlers and with Rice providing attacking fields we gradually wore them down. Taking six more wickets to finish with a career-best 13–129 from 70 overs in the match

I had set up a nine-wicket victory, but I had an unbearable fortnight of waiting in front of me.

We didn't have a game leading up to the weekend, which was set aside for the Gillette Cup final, and I knew the selectors would be meeting soon after to name their tour party. There was also an eleven-day break before the deciding Championship match against Glamorgan, punctuated only by a Sunday League match against Gloucestershire, though I made the most of that by taking 5–27 to keep my name in the headlines.

In the event the worry about the Championship was ill-founded since our opponents Glamorgan offered little resistance. Richard Hadlee did the damage as they were bowled out for 60 after we asked them to bat. We responded with 180 and with Hadlee and I taking four wickets each in their second innings the game was over with nine hours to spare. The Championship for which the county had yearned for so long was in the bag.

Finishing with 86 wickets in the Championship, and 90 in all matches, I had out-performed every other spinner in the country and, given the earlier approach from Close, I was beginning to anticipate spending the winter at places like the Taj Mahal rather than back at Trent Bridge working for the club's commercial department again. Even some of the modern game's harshest critics – the old pros who had turned to writing newspaper columns in their retirement – were screaming for me to be picked. Fred Trueman wrote in the *People*:

> 'Hemmings learned his off-spin the hard way on the featherbed wickets of Edgbaston and his accuracy makes him ideal for India',

while Denis Compton wrote in the *Sunday Express*:

> 'The transformation that has taken place in the Notts team from mediocre to best can be illustrated by the form of Eddie Hemmings. Hemmings, discarded by Warwickshire, has really

worked hard at his game and now has a belief in his own ability and has transformed this into wickets.'

Sadly, despite all the media hype, the selectors decided to take only two spinners with them to the sub-continent instead of the three normally used on the Indians' dusty wickets and England stood by the experience of Emburey and Underwood. Jim Laker, perhaps the greatest off-spinner in the history of English cricket, offered consoling words in the *Daily Express*, saying:

'Where I do take issue with the selectors is the omission of Eddie Hemmings because on this season's evidence he has developed into a better off-spin prospect than Emburey.'

I was bitterly disappointed but at the age of 32 I finally had a Championship Winners' Medal and I knew I had several years left in which to make my mark – a much brighter position than I had faced three years earlier when Warwickshire were close to throwing me on the scrapheap.

4

RON ALLSOPP – MIRACLE WORKER

During the 1980s, as Nottinghamshire began to enjoy more success than at any other time in the club's history, one harping theme was constantly raised by the critics of the county. They seemed to begrudge deeply giving us due credit for being a strong and well-balanced side that performed consistently well day in and day out at the highest level. Instead they seized on the subject of the wickets at Trent Bridge. I am sure there must have been times when our groundsman Ron Allsopp felt like issuing writs for slander and libel, yet ironically he remains one of the most open characters on the circuit when it comes to dealing with the press.

There would have been wry smiles in many quarters outside the county boundaries in August 1989 when, after we had beaten Derbyshire by 70 runs, the Test and County Cricket Board, using rules that were only introduced that season, deducted 25 points from us for a pitch that had been reported as unsatisfactory by umpires Barrie Meyer and Peter Wight.

On that occasion it was a sound judgement because on the Monday morning both captains, Tim Robinson and Kim Barnett, had been so discouraged by play on the Saturday that they agreed the umpires should ring Lord's and get permission to make history by switching pitches halfway through the game. In fact the other pitch proved to be even

33

worse and I picked up 5 for 20 in only eight overs as Derbyshire were bowled out for 64 in their second innings.

The press had a heyday, many writers claiming that Notts should have faced a similar punishment on many occasions in the 1980s, and the Notts committee, deeply embarrassed by the Lord's fine, read the riot act to Allsopp. The result was that in 1990 we played on a succession of bland pitches at Trent Bridge as he made absolutely certain there would be no further visits from the newly established TCCB flying squad of pitch inspectors. But his response only proved one thing in my opinion – that for more than a decade he had been the best groundsman in England.

As the first witness for the defence I would like to reproduce an extract from an article written shortly after we had won the Championship in 1981 by Michael Melford, who was then the highly respected cricket correspondent of the *Daily Telegraph*. He wrote:

> 'I think there is often much nonsense talked about pitches with bounce. The extra bounce is often derived simply from the effort put into it by the bowler.
>
> Rather than devalue the return of the Championship to this splendid old ground with its great, great associations after many years of small success and, in the 1950s lifeless pitches and dull cricket, one likes to think that Notts have merely prepared pitches that rewarded good bowling and batting.'

It was almost a complete myth for others regularly to claim that Trent Bridge wickets were doctored day in and day out to suit our bowlers. To my knowledge that happened only on one occasion and at the insistence of one man and that was not Allsopp.

This happened several years ago and I insist that in all my years with Notts that was the one and only occasion that a bad wicket was deliberately produced. That statement might not find too many supporters among visiting captains, who at times have wandered out at Trent Bridge to toss a coin only to discover a playing surface so green in colour that it was barely distinguishable from the rest of the square and identified only by the stumps sticking out of the ground at either end. And it is true that before his change of tack in 1990 Allsopp did leave a lot of grass on his pitches but I swear that all he ever did was produce great cricketing wickets that called for skill and left no hiding places for the mediocre player. Throughout the decade the Trent Bridge wickets had pace and bounce, which incidentally is exactly what the TCCB was looking for. The grass did provide sideways movement, but only on rare occasions could it be called excessive and to say that it was there just for Richard Hadlee was a nonsense – he didn't need it. He developed into such a fine bowler that he didn't require any extra help beyond his own skills. When he was playing with us the critics of our surfaces tended to forget that he took over 400 wickets in Test cricket where in general pitches tend to be of the highest standard, built to last five days and offering bowlers only a negligible amount of deviation.

In their own way Allsopp's wickets have always called for skill in all departments. With their pace and sure bounce a quick bowler cannot afford to stray. Anything pitched short a batsman can hook or cut with confidence knowing exactly at what height the ball is going to come through. On the other hand if a bowler over-pitches, the batsman can drive the half-volley with complete ease of mind knowing the ball will come onto the bat, not suddenly stopping and forcing him to play too early. For a paceman to succeed under such conditions unerring accuracy is vital and movement only comes from excellent technique.

For a spinner like myself the Trent Bridge wickets have rarely offered more than a slight degree of turn but that has been more than compensated for by the degree of bounce which is often just as handy as wild lateral deviation, if not more so. Plugging away on a steady line and length there is never too much reward for me if a batsman plays correctly, but woe betide anyone who gets the length of a delivery wrong. Unlike other slow wickets elsewhere the pace in the surface at Trent Bridge does not allow a batsman suddenly to realise he has misread the flight, nor does it give him time to rock onto the back foot and play the ball out square on either side of the wicket.

The bounce normally responds to an ill-judged forward prod by rapping the batsman on the gloves and in the early 1980s I could not have had a better man standing at short leg for Notts than Basher Hassan. I would estimate that he was worth an extra 15 to 20 wickets for me every season. He was undoubtedly fearless, though not reckless to the extent that he would place himself in a position where he might get hit and seriously hurt. Season in and season out he would always feature somewhere near the top when the figures were produced showing the leading catchers in the country. But it was not so much the catches that he took, but his mere presence and reputation standing there menacingly three or four yards from the batsmen, that made them think. If they were not bobbing up catches in his direction then they were desperately trying to think of other ways to play, making mistakes, and I would pick up their wickets some-where else.

Playing cricket at Trent Bridge is very much a matter of having the right mental approach. I remember the days when Mike Brearley used to arrive with his strong Middlesex side and while he may have been dismayed by the sight of another green surface he never let on, he would just say, 'Well that's what we have have got to play on, let's get on with it.' But then there have been the opposite sort – the typical moaner who even before he has strapped on his pads declares there is no way he can score runs on that sort of surface. In that frame of mind, one might just as well not bother going out to the crease.

If playing conditions at Trent Bridge over the years that I have played there have been as bad as some would like to make out, then would one of the many critics answer one simple question: how on earth over that period did we manage to produce two top-class batsmen in Tim Robinson and Chris Broad, who far from being shellshocked day in and day out, developed into opening batsmen at Test level, with records that stood the test alongside anyone else tried by England and were a lot better than most apart from perhaps Graham Gooch?

During our peak years Allsopp was an integral part of our success but he was only regularly producing the type of wickets that were the envy of other counties. Indeed others in the mid-1980s began to try to leave some grass on their pitches in an attempt to achieve the same effect but without his ability to produce true and hard surfaces underneath. It was their failures which probably caused much more alarm at Lord's but because Notts as a side began to be so successful the finger of blame was always pointed in our direction.

Above and beyond being able to call upon the services of the country's top groundsman people also seemed to forget that Notts went through most of the decade with a well-balanced side which perhaps only Middlesex to begin with and later Worcestershire and Essex could match for all-round strength. In Broad, Robinson and Randall we had three batsmen of proven Test calibre. In Clive Rice we had an aggressive captain. In Rice and Richard Hadlee we had two world-class all-rounders, or to put it more simply, two batsmen and two team bowlers who needed just two places in the side between them. Backing up the bowlers we had an England wicketkeeper in Bruce French who might have played many more than sixteen Tests had it not been for cruel luck with injury. I will not blow my own trumpet but needless to say we were not short in the spinning department either since we also extracted the best out of Mike Bore after Yorkshire unwisely decided they no longer had a use for his services.

5
THE REALISATION OF DREAMS

My father Ted found himself presented with a bill for £127 halfway through July 1982 as the result of a promise he had made to me some sixteen years earlier. When I joined the Warwickshire staff initially as an all-rounder, Dad gave me an incentive to do well by saying he would pay me £1 for every run I scored in my maiden first-class century. But for years he had been able to hang onto his money as I had passed 50 on several occasions without ever going on to make the big one.

I finally reached the elusive three figures when Yorkshire arrived at Worksop to find us in some state of disarray having lost our three previous Championship games. There was no sign of the bad trot ending as Arnie Sidebottom tore into our top order with the result that when I went in at number nine to join Bruce French we were in deep trouble at 127 for 7. While French and, later, Nigel Illingworth and Kevin Cooper held Yorkshire at bay at the other end I set about repairing our innings. The century took me a shade over three hours and among the six and fourteen fours none felt sweeter than the straight drive to the ropes off Graham Stevenson that took me to the hundred. Dad's bill would have been even bigger, but having taken our score to 329 at the close of the first day, Rice declared overnight.

Unfortunately Yorkshire, chasing 305 in their second innings, went on to win the match by two wickets as our chances of retaining the title slipped further from our reach. However the month of July was one of immense personal achievement since straight from the Yorkshire match we travelled down to Lord's to meet Somerset in the Benson and Hedges Cup final, but even more importantly a fortnight earlier I had finally received the long-awaited call from the selectors.

Although I had been taking wickets steadily since the start of the season I had not bowled as many overs as in 1981. Phil Edmonds had played in all three Tests in the first of the summer's series against the Indians with Geoff Miller winning one cap when the selectors opted to take an off-spinner into the second Test at Old Trafford. But my call-up came for the Prudential Trophy one-day games against Pakistan and the prospect of playing in the first match, which was to be staged before my home crowd at Trent Bridge, made it even more exciting.

Before the game I met Jim Laker for the first time and he offered me a quiet word of advice. 'Always try to spin the ball all the time, even if it is a good wicket,' he said and I thought if that was good enough for him it would be good enough for me too. My introduction to cricket at the highest level, however, was not the easiest. The ground was packed out and I had never played in front of a crowd of more than 7,000 before. When Bob Willis asked me to bowl, Mudassar Nazar and Mohsin Khan were striking the ball all over the park in a century opening stand, with one particularly confident Mudassar shot smashing a window in the Trent Bridge restaurant.

I was so nervous that I never thought the ball was going to leave my hand and I took some punishment in my first two overs, conceding 12 runs. Then I got the break we badly needed. Mohsin came down the wicket to play a straight drive. Although I fielded the ball cleanly, Mudassar had moved out of his ground at the bowler's end and I threw down the stumps to run him out. I didn't actually get a wicket in my eleven overs, but after my poor start I was happy to concede only 45 runs and in the deep I picked up a catch off Ian Botham's bowling to dismiss Wasim Raja and we eventually won by seven wickets.

The second encounter at Old Trafford saw Botham and Mike Gatting set up a big England score when they put on 84 together in only eleven overs en route to us scoring 295 for 8. Given our overall bowling performance at Nottingham that was always going to be a daunting target for the Pakistanis, although they made quite an effort, especially Wasim Raja who struck me for two sixes in one over. They, however, were the only blemishes on a tight bowling performance which saw me give away only 18 more runs in my eleven overs and also bowl their experienced wicketkeeper Wasim Bari to claim my first international scalp.

It was to be more than a week before the selectors were due to name their side for the first Test at Edgbaston but my hopes were kept high after skipper Bob Willis talked about my one-day performances to the press saying, 'Hemmings was under a lot of pressure. There is a fair amount of competition for the spinner's role and he took his opportunity with both hands.' I filled in the gap before the Test team was announced by scoring that maiden hundred and appearing at Lord's in the final with barely a moment to think about England.

The call came the morning after our Lord's defeat and the statisticians quickly worked out that at the age of 33 England had picked only two bowlers older than me – Robin Jackman and Ian Thomson – to make their debuts since the Second World War. The fact that the Test was to be played at Edgbaston, just four years after my leaving Warwickshire, added a bit more spice. Although I felt few hard feelings towards the club since moving to Nottingham it was turning out to be the best possible thing which could have happened to my career.

With England batting first my opening contribution to

English Test cricket was hardly outstanding as, batting at nine, I fell lbw to Imram Khan, having scored only two in our total of 272. But I only needed four balls on the second day to record my first wicket as Javed Miandad tried to hit me out of the ground but merely succeeded in skying a catch to Willis at wide mid-on. Although Edgbaston was expected to help batsmen through the game it turned out to be a low-scoring match. I also got the wicket of Mansoor Akhtar as we earned a first-innings lead of 21, and then contributed a useful 19 in our second dig before Pakistan were asked to score 313 to win. The fact that they failed by 133 was almost entirely due to Botham who took 4–70 on our way to victory but since I chipped in with the wicket of their number three Tahir Naqqash I did my bit, and furthermore it was a spectacular dismissal, the cameras catching me in mid-air diving full strength to take a left-handed return catch.

Figuring in three wins in my first three England games gave me great satisfaction, but I was soon brought down to earth when having been selected for the second Test at Lord's we were thumped by ten wickets. The experience also taught me never to take selection for granted for I was dropped as a result of the defeat. We had been handicapped at the start of the match when Willis dropped out through injury and his successor David Gower was left with an attack consisting almost entirely of medium-pacers with Ian Greig, Robin Jackman and Derek Pringle supporting Botham. Batting first, Pakistan made 428 for 8 declared and we were forced to follow on when we could make only 227 in reply.

The news that I was not in the side for the third Test incensed Clive Rice who wrote in the *Trent Bridge News*:

'The axing of Eddie Hemmings from the Test team is very disappointing, not only to me, but I am sure to all Nottingham-shire. I don't think there is any point in getting too upset, as this sort of treatment seems to be the "norm" of the England selectors over the years. That now leads me to my second point about building up players' confidence and then smashing it in order that they might have a so-called look at another player. Eddie is the type of player that needs confidence. He left Warwickshire with little confidence and since then he has blossomed into an international player. All this is due to him gaining belief in himself which leads back to his confidence in Nottinghamshire and our confidence in him. I wonder how much trust he has in the selectors now?'

Rice later added, 'Eddie, you would still be in my side for the Australia tour and I do hope the selectors come to their senses.'

The selectors chose to have 'a look at' Vic Marks as England won the third Test and the series at Leeds, but that was hardly conclusive since he only bowled two overs, although they included the wicket of a tail-ender Sikander Bakht. While that match was being played, Geoff Miller and I were involved in a pretty inconclusive comparison of our skills as Notts played Derbyshire at Trent Bridge. In the end when the selectors named the tour party in mid September all three of us won places and while it was the fulfilment of another of my ambitions, the selectors took more stick for including three off-spinners, leaving out both the slow left-arm specialists, Edmonds and Nick Cook.

In the weeks leading up to the departure for Australia I accepted an invitation from Rohan Khanhai to go to the West Indies for the second year running to play in the Jamaica International Cricket Festival. It was an ideal trip to keep my mind from dwelling too much on the prospects of going on my first major England tour; it was also a good opportunity for keeping myself fit.

After playing a one-day game against the Island in Montego Bay we flew down to Kingston for a four-day match against a West Indies XI that was virtually at Test strength, but what should have been a showpiece game was almost wrecked by heavy rain. That may have disappointed the locals but it was to present me with my one and only ten-wicket haul.

Had it been a Test or a competitive first-class match I doubt whether the game would have started at all. The continuous rain leading up to the match had seeped under the covers and left a wet strip right across the wicket at one end and there was little hope of it drying out. But being a Festival match the two captains John Wright and Clive Lloyd agreed to play on the strict understanding that only spinners would operate from one end. Thus after we had been bowled out for 262 I was resigned to bowling a long spell under a by now burning sun just to make sure there was some cricket for the crowd. The damp patch was on a seamer's length, far too short to be of any use to me, while the wicket on my length was as good as any for batting though there was a useful bit of bounce. In the event the West Indies side, with little to play for bar entertainment, went for their shots and one by one presented my fielders with a series of catches. Trevor Jesty in particular took two fine boundary catches, but my heart went out to a young Jamaican lad who had been loaned to us as twelfth man. He took two very good catches to get rid of Lawrence Rowe and Malcolm Marshall, but he had been fielding in front of a section of the crowd where some fans had clearly tasted too much of the local Red Stripe beer and they responded by pelting him with bottles. For his own safety we moved him after that to a spot in front of the Members' Stand where the occupants were clearly in a more sober frame of mind.

I have to say that I was helped by the general attacking nature of the West Indies batsmen and the lack of pressure they were under in a match that was heading in no other direction than towards a draw. Nevertheless the scorecard made happy reading.

Apart from the obvious pleasure, which helped me over the tiredness of bowling nearly 50 overs on the trot, the ten-wicket haul had little significance at the time; after all we

International XI 262 (G Fowler 63 C J Richards 62;
S T Clarke 5 for 26)

West Indies XI:

C G Greenidge c Ghavri b Hemmings	43
D L Haynes c Butcher b Hemmings	96
G Powell c Richards b Hemmings	16
L G Rowe c sub b Hemmings	47
P J Dujon c Jesty b Hemmings	19
C H Lloyd c Jesty b Hemmings	60
M D Marshall c sub b Hemmings	40
R C Haynes c Wright b Hemmings	15
A M E Roberts st Richards b Hemmings	34
S T Clarke b Hemmings	6
M A Holding not out	3
Extras (b 18, 1b 11, w 1, nb 10)	40
Total	419

Fall of wickets: 1/98 2/137 3/198 4/254 5/261 6/353 7/369 8/400 9/414
Bowling: Allott 24–6–70–0 Ghavri 17–1–70–0
Hemmings 49.3–14–175–10 Jarvis 16–2–45–0 Jesty 7–1–19–0

had only been playing a Festival game. It was only months later, back in England during the 1983 season, that I learned that the match had been granted first-class status and that my achievement would enter the record books.

It was certainly not the first time that a bowler had run through a complete innings. *Wisden* showed the feat had been achieved on 71 occasions previously stretching back to the first recorded instance in 1848. But it did stand out for two reasons, one of which made me proud, the other I like conveniently to forget. It was only the second time it had been achieved in the Caribbean, and was the first instance by a spinner. But my haul of 10–175 turned out to be the most expensive of all time, by some margin – in fact I had conceded 45 more runs than Kent's Titch Freeman playing against Lancashire at Maidstone in 1929. Furthermore only Jim Laker who needed 51.2 overs in his historic dismissal of the Australians at Old Trafford in 1956 had bowled more overs to complete the task.

News of the achievement had already been digested in Australia by the time we arrived Down Under in mid October and while several local critics thought that form might win me a Test place I knew it was not going to be that easy. Although John Emburey and Derek Underwood had both ruled themselves out of Test cricket for three years after taking part in the rebel South African tour six months earlier, there had still been considerable competition for the spinners' places in the party. There was general surprise that the selectors had made three spaces available for slow bowlers rather than the two normally taken to Australia and by picking me, Miller and Marks they had opted for three off spinners. Perhaps Edmonds would have offered more variety since the previous summer with Middlesex he had taken 71 wickets with his slow left-arm spin.

There were rumours that Bob Willis didn't particularly want a strong outspoken character like Phil in his dressing room. In fact Bob and I had not been the greatest of mutual admirers during our years together at Warwickshire. But who was I to argue? I was on my first tour and despite the competition for places I intended to make the most of it, however limited the opportunities.

Miller and Marks played in the opening first-class fixture against Queensland at Brisbane and poor Vic's reputation suffered a dreadful blow when Harry Frie, a robust character with an outback personality, decided to take him apart scoring 50 from only 24 balls in the Queensland first innings with 38 of them coming from two of Marks' overs. Thereafter the Australian crowds everywhere dismissed Marks' ability, but he answered all his critics four years later when he surprisingly signed to play for one winter with Western Australia. As they won the Sheffield Shield he took 30 wickets, made two half-centuries and several useful 40s to take their Player of the Year Award.

But after one game of the tour he had slipped down the selectors' ratings while I did my own chances of playing in the first Test no harm at all as we moved down the coast – well not exactly. First we flew south on a jet to Sydney and then transferred to a light aircraft to travel back in the opposite direction – to Newcastle for a three-day non-first-class match against Northern New South Wales.

Our opposition was not the strongest with only Rick McCosker and Gus Gilmour having played Test cricket and four other players who had featured in the odd game for New South Wales. But with a helpful wicket I picked up 5–38 as they were bowled out for 163 and after Chris Tavare had scored a fluent 157 to give us a good lead I got 4–30 to set us up for a morale-boosting ten-wicket win.

It was only ever likely that England would play one spinner at the most in the first Test at Perth which was still two weeks away, and while I had made my mark with the ball the selectors still seemed likely to prefer Miller in the side because of his ability to bat at number seven – and our long tail was going to need some protecting in the series which lay ahead. My hopes therefore rose when we played South Australia.

The Adelaide Oval may be one of the prettiest grounds in Australia with views over the nearby botanical gardens and several church spires towering over the outfield, but the wicket can be a nightmare for bowlers. With Willis suffering from a virus we were led by Botham who chose to bat first on winning the toss; this virtually gave me a day off as the top order batsmen all scored a few. But it was straight into the fray the next morning as we subsided to 380 for 9, but I took the opportunity to prove to the selectors that I could score runs when they were needed. For the last wicket Jackman and I, despite a fairly consistent barrage of short-pitched bowling, added 112. It was only the third time in all the tours of Australia that an English tenth-wicket pair had passed the hundred mark, and I completed my own half-century in 66 minutes. I had added ten more and neither

Robin nor I looked in any trouble when Botham made his declaration.

By the end of the day I thought I had done enough to guarantee my place in the Perth Test in a twelve-over spell which despite the many spaces on the vast Oval outfield cost just 19 runs and included two wickets. The figures looked even more impressive once we had bowled the South Australians out for 344 since I had by then bowled 44 overs without a break and taken 4–102. It was only in the second innings when South Australia were chasing 375 in four hours that the wicket began to turn and although I failed to clinch us a victory I was certain that three more wickets to go with my runs would get me the vote ahead of Miller, especially since he was suffering from a shoulder injury.

I was duly named in the twelve for our final warm-up game against Western Australia in Perth, but on the morning of the game Miller got the nod ahead of me and I knew that I didn't figure in the selectors' plans. I was bitterly disappointed because the WA match was being used as a full-scale practice for the Test and, although Miller didn't bowl in the game because the green and damp wicket was tailor-made for our pacemen, he did score an unbeaten 39 in our first innings, which sealed my fate.

Although the Australians lost the services of Terry Alderman for the rest of the winter after he was injured rugby-tackling a spectator, we were happy with our draw from the first Test, but since I had done no bowling for a fortnight while kicking my heels as twelfth man I was rusty and slightly frustrated by the time we went to Sydney to face New South Wales. Spinners rely so heavily on rhythm when they are at the top of their form and without the constant action it is hard just to settle into a steady line and length.

The lay-off probably accounted for my disappointing showing in the New South Wales first innings but on the final day of the game when they threatened to score 333 for victory, David Gower, who was leading the side in the absence of Willis, gave me 22 overs on the trot. I grabbed five wickets – all the victims being Test players – as we won by 26 runs. With 23 wickets under my belt from only three games on tour, far more than any other bowler, I felt sure I would make the Brisbane side.

The Test ended up as a double disappointment as we lost by seven wickets and I suffered a groin strain which considerably hampered my bowling. As the Australians eased their way past a victory target of 190 on the final day the only consolation for me was bowling Keppler Wessels and getting Allan Border brilliantly caught at slip by Ian Botham. Later on in the tour, however, we returned to Brisbane for a one-day international which at least gives me one smile to remember the city by.

During the match the action came to an abrupt halt when a spectator released a young pig onto the field with the word 'Botham' painted on the right-hand side of its stomach and 'Eddie' on the other – a rather cutting reference to the two biggest girths in the England touring party! I felt a twinge of sympathy for the animal since we later learned it had been smuggled past the security men on the gate inside an 'eski' normally used for keeping cans of beer cold. But it was a great example of the way Australian crowds really go in for their sport.

Since the Packer revolution the hype for Australian cricket has been immense with a constant stream of television advertisements building up the home side into world-beating supermen and generally dismissing the opposition in terms which are not always complimentary. That mood has transferred itself to the fans and although it was my first visit Down Under I had quickly learned that you have to have a fairly thick skin on the field. They are always ready with the witty remark, though they also greatly appreciate any player who gives back as good as he gets.

I found that I had a good rapport with the 'Aussies' on the field and life was certainly different off it. With all the

games so heavily advertised it was impossible to go anywhere in the streets without being recognised, whereas back
home, even in Nottingham, I could go shopping in a super-
market with Chris and the boys and not one head would
turn in our direction. I enjoyed the Australian style and since
the hype was attracting fans to the games it wasn't bad for
the cricket – despite the extra pressure, I prefer playing in
front of a full crowd rather than rows and rows of seats any
day of the week, even if the jibes are sometimes a bit close
to the knuckle. As for the Pig, I reckoned that since the fans
had printed Botham's surname on one side but been familiar
enough to use my Christian name, I must be one up in the
popularity stakes!

Bob Willis did his best to keep team morale high, saying
that the defeat in Brisbane was not the end of the world,
but as our shuttle tour of Australia took us on to Melbourne
for a state game against Victoria my groin strain problems
were compounded by a stiff shoulder and I was given the
match off to make sure I was fully fit for the third Test in
Adelaide. I was grateful that the pool at the Melbourne
Hilton is a very inviting place to relax. The shoulder was
still giving me slight problems as the third Test got under
way, with Willis making the fatal mistake of asking the
Australians to bat first. He had spotted dampness in the
pitch 24 hours before the game but by the time the Aussies
got to work on it it had dried into a perfect batting strip
and they made hay, scoring 265 for 3 on the first day.

We were only really in the game for the first two sessions
on the second day during which time I completed a mara-
thon spell of 46 overs. They only yielded the wicket of David
Hookes, but by tying the batsmen down at one end I allowed
our pacemen to attack from the other with the result that
the last seven Australian wickets went down while only a
further 160 runs were added. Given the state of the pitch
we had only ourselves to blame as we were then bowled out
for 216 and after being forced to follow on lost by eight

wickets. My contribution with the bat hardly impressed the side as I was bowled by Jeff Thomson in the first innings and caught at short-square-leg off Geoff Lawson in the second without troubling the scorer on either occasion and facing a total of only six deliveries.

Defeat left us 2–0 down in the series and with a mountain to climb if we were going to hang on to the Ashes – I wonder to this day whether Willis realised that on the nine previous occasions an English captain had chosen to field first in Australia only one game had ended with a victory, the other eight all resulting in heavy defeats.

As Christmas approached we headed across to Tasmania for two fixtures and all the signs pointed to my place being in danger. I didn't play in either of the Island games and as the Boxing Day Test date with the Aussies back in Melbourne approached I could see I was heading for another lay-off. My three wickets in two Tests had cost 225 runs, even though I had conceded only just over two runs an over, and I was averaging only eleven with the bat. Miller on the other hand had taken five wickets at 31 apiece, was averaging 19, and since history suggested we would need a full complement of seamers at the MCG I consoled myself with the thought that Chris and the boys would be joining me over the festive period.

Although I was on the sidelines, the fourth Test turned out to be an epic in which Norman Cowans, with the tour nearly three months old, finally justified his inclusion as the young and aspiring fast bowler in the party. He took six wickets as the Aussies chased 292 for victory but it was Ian Botham who finally scraped us home on the last morning of the game. Allan Border and Jeff Thomson had almost pulled a remarkable victory out of the hat for the Australians taking their fourth-innings score from a desperate 218 for 9 to within a single boundary of their target in a defiant last-wicket stand. But a bit of Botham magic found the edge of Thomson's bat and while Chris Tavare could only palm up a sharp chance at slip Miller ran around behind him to complete the catch and clinch our three-run victory.

Winning at Melbourne put us in great heart and we arrived in Sydney for the final Test knowing that if we could win again we would square the series and hold onto the Ashes. Although in my two Tests on the tour up to that point I had only taken three wickets at a cost of over 70 runs apiece, the tour selectors took one look at the Sydney pitch and decided once again that we should go in with two spinners, so I was preferred to Derek Pringle in the attack.

While I was delighted to get another chance there was a slight flaw in the team's thinking. While Sydney later in the 1980s was to see a series of Test matches decided by the spinners it hadn't yet developed the reputation for turning square, and although there were bare patches on the wicket the locals, who knew Sydney better than we did, insisted that the surface often played better than its appalling appearance would suggest. Noticeably the Australians only included one spinner, Bruce Yardley, in their line-up and when Greg Chappell won the toss and chose to bat first it would need something extraordinary in the nature of a follow-on by England for us to bowl last and make maximum use of a wearing wicket.

Looking back there can be little doubt that the Ashes series was settled in the first over of the match. Off the last ball, before the Aussies had even made the scoreboard tick over, Keppler Wessels called John Dyson for a sharp single and although Bob Willis, fielding off his own bowling, threw down the stumps with Dyson out of his ground, umpire Mel Johnson gave the batsman the benefit of the doubt. He claimed later that since Dyson was moving at full pace he could not tell whether he was six inches in or out of his crease at the time the wicket was broken, but our disappointment was compounded on two fronts. Television replays showed that Dyson was not even in the same picture as the crease when Bob's throw found its target – a view confirmed by freeze-framed photographs on the front pages of some Australian papers the next morning. Furthermore Dyson went on to score 79 before I had him caught behind by Bob Taylor, and that turned out to be two runs more than Australia's crucial first-innings lead of 77.

Although the wicket did begin to turn as the Australian second innings got under way it was certainly not vicious, but again we found ourselves undone by what we thought was a harsh umpiring decision. This time it concerned Kim Hughes, who was set to take over their captaincy during the World Series Cup that was to follow. A combination of myself, Willis and Ian Botham had dragged us right back into the match by reducing the Australians to 82 for 3. And it might have been four down soon after when Hughes clipped Geoff Miller off his boot into the hands of Geoff Cook at short-leg. Despite our frantic appeals the umpire's finger stayed down and Hughes stayed on to score 137 and leave us with the monumental task of scoring a world record 460 in 375 minutes to win the match and retain the Ashes.

The Australian second innings was a war of attrition between their batsmen, Miller and me as we two spinners bowled nearly 100 overs between us. I picked up 3 for 116 from 46 overs which, added to my first innings 3 for 68, gave me a return of 6 for 184, easily my best for England up to that point. But by the time our second innings began with half an hour of the fourth day remaining I was knackered, ready to put my feet up and enjoy a long cool beer at the end of the day's play.

You can imagine my surprise when, as Geoff Cook and Chris Tavare were about to go out and begin our second knock, Willis strode over to me in the dressing room and asked if I would be prepared to stand by as nightwatchman. This was totally unusual because Bob Taylor had performed the duty well, without too many blunders or any complaints, throughout the tour, whereas I had never done it in my life before. I couldn't see any logical reason for the change, though in our first innings while Taylor had fallen lbw to Thomson for a duck, I had hung around making 29, adding useful runs in a stand of 50 in as many minutes for our eighth wicket with Miller.

I didn't argue with Willis' decision, but I had barely strapped on my pads when in our second over Cook fell lbw to Geoff Lawson and I found myself dragging my weary legs to the crease. I don't know whether I saw the first ball from Lawson better than usual but it was just short of a length and I went onto the back foot and quite out of character with my normal front-footed style cracked it over the tops of the covers for three. Although Tavare took the next couple of overs I ended up facing the last few balls of the day and with the help of a rather lucky inside edge which streaked away down the leg side to the boundary I ended up seven not out overnight.

When play began on the final morning Chappell crowded me with fielders, but with the result that he left plenty of gaps on the Sydney outfield and my confidence began to grow as I played several shots through them gradually building a decent score. The fours, however, persuaded the Aussies to move their field back and an early blow on the hand made batting more difficult. But just as I had completed my first ever Test 50 I got hit on the hand again and that was a telling blow; I had broken a bone.

I went to lunch at 54 not out but since we had lost Tavare and David Gower, the latter falling to a remarkable catch at deep mid-off by David Hookes, there was still a lot of work to be done to save the Test match. For nearly an hour in the afternoon I continued to make steady if painful progress and while I was eventually out for 95 it still rankles that I was robbed of probably my best chance to make 100 in a Test, an Ashes one at that. Having scored my maiden first-class century for Notts just months beforehand it would have made a fantastic double inside twelve months. The umpire judged that I was caught behind by Rod Marsh off

Yardley, but I swear I never hit the ball. It pitched in the rough and caught both of my pads but when I got home at the end of the tour and put the video on freeze frame it is quite clear that my bat did not make contact.

The innings proved to a lot of people that I could bat and the problem had been for so long that batting down the order at eight the chances of making a big score are few and far between. Let's face it, if it's a good wicket the top-order batsmen all pile in and there's a declaration – and if it's a bad one there is no reason why I should succeed where the others above me have failed. It was nice to have an opportunity in Sydney to play a long innings and even more satisfying to know that I didn't give a chance in 195 minutes at the crease. It was a genuine innings and I was upset that I didn't get the other five, but that's the way the game goes. I was upset but if the umpire says you are out that's it and off you go.

By then we were well on the way to saving the match, since the victory target had been far too stiff to be a realistic proposition. But when the game ended in a draw the Australian supporters surged around the famous old pavilion at Sydney, which has been retained despite the building of magnificent new stands on either side, as their players began to celebrate winning the Ashes. Champagne by the gallon and more than the odd case of XXXX flowed in the opposition dressing room, but there was near silence in ours. I couldn't help reflecting on the injustices in the game. Had Dyson been given run out or the umpire accepted that Hughes had been caught at short-leg we might well have won while I had been robbed of that most coveted prize – an Ashes Test century – by a decision that had gone the other way.

The Ashes lost, it was time for the triangular World Series Cup in which New Zealand were the third team involved. But with the doctors discovering that I had broken a small bone in the back of my right hand I wasn't considered for our opening six games. By the time we returned to Sydney late in January for the seventh of the ten qualifying games we were under pressure to qualify for the finals having lost four games, three of them to the Aussies.

The selectors had decided that we looked at our strongest when we played two spinners in the Cup games and since Miller was suffering from an elbow injury and my hand had almost completely recovered I got a place in the side. So too did Jackman who had long since been dubbed the Lord Lucan of the touring party. Jackers, after a distinguished seam bowling career with Surrey that stretched back to 1964, had waited a long time for his recognition by England and in fact was about to announce his retirement from the game when the selectors picked him for the tour. Up to that point, however, he had not been selected for either the Tests or the one-day games and in fact because of our programme had not played any cricket since before Christmas.

The alterations to our attack paid handsome dividends. After mid-afternoon rain had reduced the contest to 41 overs a side we made 207 and for a time the Aussies looked like making mincemeat of that target before Jackman and I induced a quite dramatic collapse. In the space of seven balls he accounted for Hughes, Greg Chappell and Keppler Wessels before I finished off the innings with the wickets of Rod Marsh, Dennis Lillee and John Maguire. They had lost their last eight wickets for only 37 runs and our 98-run victory put us back in the hunt for the finals.

The following weekend in Adelaide we took on New Zealand on one of the hottest days of cricket I can ever recall – it was well over 100 degrees in the shade. After my performance in Sydney I kept my place in the side and with Ian Botham beginning our innings with a blistering 65 in an opening stand of 75 with Tavare and later Gower playing at his elegant best we ran up the massive score of 296 for 5 from our 50 overs. Since the Kiwis needed to break one-day records to overtake that target we were confident of victory especially as they had only made 33 by the time their most experienced batsmen Glenn Turner and Geoff Howarth were back in the pavilion. But then things started to go drastically wrong. I bowled six overs which cost 49 runs and included a dropped catch, Botham went for 61 off 8 and Trevor Jesty got a hammering too as New Zealand achieved the impossible with the luxury of seven balls to spare.

Willis had warned us against complacency in the break between innings and when we returned to the dressing room he let fly with all barrels blazing. I kept my place against Australia the following day bowling much more tidily as we won by 14 runs but when we travelled to Perth for our final game against the Kiwis, which we lost by seven wickets to miss out on the final, the selectors decided to play Norman Cowans – an extra seamer – in my place. That signalled the end of my tour and the start of a four-year period when the selectors looked elsewhere for the services of an off spinner.

After a short trip to New Zealand for three meaningless one-day internationals played by a very jaded England side, I returned home still suffering slightly from the hand injury but with the added complication that my shoulder muscle injury was getting worse and it was to plague me for a year. Although I had not had an outstanding tour in Australia I didn't feel the trip had gone too badly for me either, but others who mattered clearly felt differently.

An operation on the shoulder would have prevented me touring New Zealand and Pakistan the following winter, but when in 1984 Surrey's Pat Pocock was selected to join Gower's 1984–85 tour to India, I knew that the road back to the England team, if I was ever going to make it, would be a long hard slog. In the summer of 1984 I had been the leading slow bowler in the country with 94 wickets at 23.61 runs apiece, but I was overlooked in favour of Pat Pocock who was then 38 years of age and had taken only 63 wickets at 25.71. And when Gower returned triumphant from India with a 2–1 victory in the series and started preparing for the 1985 Ashes series, John Emburey was once again available having served his three-year ban for joining the 1982 rebel tour.

6

IN THE FRAME
1981–90

Given that there are four domestic competitions open to the counties every summer it is amazing to realise that between the years of 1981 and 1987 not one trophy came to Trent Bridge. Of course Notts did not have a divine right to the silverware above the other sixteen first-class counties, but as the rebuilding of the team which started under Ken Taylor in 1979 continued and our playing strength increased so too did our expectations. With one exception, season in and season out we were always there or thereabouts, we were playing exciting cricket and involved in many high-tension matches and yet were to spend several years as the 'bridesmaids' of English cricket.

I hate using the expression, but at times it seemed that luck was against us; we simply didn't get the right chances, particularly on the injury front. Although the Championship pennant was flying over the ground at the start of the 1982 season, the committee had added to the fire power of our seam attack during the winter by signing the former England seamer Mike Hendrick from Derbyshire. It was a mouth-watering prospect for our fans to see Richard Hadlee and Clive Rice roaring in with the new ball and to know that even if the batsmen coped with their initial fire, Hendrick, with his reputation as one of the meanest bowlers in the English game, would be there to come on first change and tie them down with his unerring accuracy.

The reality, however, turned out to be very different. Hadlee, plagued by a succession of injuries, bowled only half the overs he had managed in 1981, Rice began to suffer from a neck injury that limited him to just 75 overs in the season while Hendrick played in only nine games, all of them in the first half of the season.

With so much planned for the trio it was ironic that they played together in only one match – the Benson and Hedges Cup final in July – and we managed to make a complete hash of it. We had only just scraped into the club's first-ever final at Lord's when Hadlee rescued us from the brink of disaster in the semi-finals against Lancashire. With all the top-class bowlers at our disposal we were quite capable of giving Somerset a run for their money in the final despite the reputations of Joel Garner, Viv Richards and Ian Botham. But for the attack to be of any use we needed a decent number of runs on the board batting first so, when we were all out for 130 in 50.1 overs the match was a write-off as a meaningful contest.

The club's problems with the pace attack were compounded elsewhere as Mike Bore was only available for six games with injuries and I went missing, albeit happily, for most of a month after receiving my first England recognition against Pakistan. That we were able to finish the season in fourth place in the Championship was no mean feat and a tribute to the way we managed to patch the side together, at times under difficult circumstances.

Although that summer began to see the emergence of two highly promising young batsmen in Paul Johnson and Tim Robinson, the county underwent a cost-cutting exercise in the winter releasing two other youngsters, Ian Pont and Neil Weightman. With the vastly experienced Bob White and Paul Todd also deciding to leave the staff, our resources were stretched thinly in 1983 and we paid a heavy penalty.

I had returned from a winter spent with England in Australia and New Zealand suffering from a torn muscle in my bowling shoulder. In early April after a month's rest it felt better but it was not completely healed and once the weekly routine of county cricket got under way it became an increasing problem. I had been hoping that the experience of touring and playing Test cricket would make me an even better bowler at county level but, hampered by the shoulder, my form suffered. In late June I did manage one shattering burst at Trent Bridge which bowled Lancashire out for 65 and my figures of 7–23 were considered a career best – and they remained so until about a month later when the news finally reached me that the ten-wicket haul in Jamaica the previous autumn had been recognised as first-class.

But that was a rare bright spot in an otherwise bleak summer. As Hadlee was away on duty with the touring New Zealanders and Rice's bad neck deteriorated to the extent that he didn't bowl a single ball, the onus was left on me and Hendrick, who had at least recovered to bowl over 550 overs in the Championship.

I knew as the months went on that the shoulder would need surgery, but while there was still an outside chance that England might seek my services again, and with Notts struggling to field a strong attack, I was determined to see the summer out. I had also so often in the past seen players come back from a winter tour complaining about one problem or another, putting on a bit of an act, and I didn't want to be regarded in a dim light. At first the pain wasn't too bad and I thought if I ignored it, it might go away, but by the end of the season, in which I got through more than 800 overs in all, I was bowling with a makeshift action that reduced my effectiveness completely. It was no wonder that we only finished fourteenth in the Championship and joint bottom of the Sunday League and made very little progress in the two knockout competitions.

Once the season was over I underwent a series of medical tests. Eventually it was decided that an operation could not be avoided and it was carried out in early January 1984. I then spent three months kicking my heels around the house while the scars healed and was able to train lightly when the team reported back for the new season. There was one new face in our line-up with the close season signing of Chris Broad, who felt a move to Trent Bridge from Gloucestershire might improve his England chances, which it did. And while Rice was to begin to start bowling again during the season, the availability once more of Hadlee meant our seam attack would be almost back to full strength.

It turned out to be an incredible summer for all of us at Trent Bridge and it was almost beyond belief that at the end of a thrilling five months we finished up empty-handed. Most people's memories of that year revolve around Hadlee, who, playing in all of our 24 Championship fixtures, became the first player since Fred Titmus in 1967 to complete 'the double', taking 117 wickets and scoring 1,179 runs. The size of that achievement was put into perspective by the fact that the Championship programme had been reduced from 28 matches in 1969 and in the intervening fifteen years only five players had achieved the reduced double of 1,000 runs and 75 wickets.

Much was made at the time of Hadlee's meticulously planned campaign and he carried it out to the letter. That was very much the attitude of the man at the time. He was a single-minded professional and we all admired his cricket, but in the dressing room he was not so much unpopular as sometimes distant from the rest of us and I used to wonder whether his campaigns were planned purely for his own benefit or matched up to the needs of the side. In terms of a more global outlook Rice seemed much more aware.

I used to wind Rice up by saying that AC Smith at Warwickshire had been the best skipper I had ever played under, though it was not necessarily the case, and in my early years we established quite a fiery relationship. I am sure that for his part Rice had worked out just how to get the best out of me and that was by winding me up in return. We often used to have arguments on the pitch over the placing of fielders when both of us appeared to dig our heels in and the language was fairly spicy, but he knew I would perform at my best when the adrenalin was really buzzing. Sometimes I am sure he deliberately rubbed me up the wrong way so that I would bowl my heart out to try to prove him wrong. For several seasons we existed like that and the formula worked, though by the end of his time at Trent Bridge, when he felt that he had learned all there was to know about captaincy, I thought he started to become dictatorial.

But while Rice bowled just over 200 overs in 1984 there was a tremendous amount of aggression in his captaincy and by scoring over 1,500 runs alongside Hadlee in the middle order we were rarely dismissed for small totals. Three other batsmen scored over 1,000 that summer – Robinson passing the mark for the first time and forming an opening partnership with Broad that was to pose a threat to opening bowlers all around the country and indeed the world at Test level for several years.

The final days of my recuperation from the shoulder operation forced me to miss the first two games of the season, and by early June I only had seven wickets at a cost of 43 runs apiece. That all changed when Glamorgan visited Trent Bridge and I took 6–50, then followed up with a twelve-wicket haul in a home game against Gloucestershire. In August as we gradually closed on Essex at the top of the table I achieved a hat-trick for only the second time in my career, removing David Capel, David Steele and George Sharp with three successive balls at Trent Bridge and by the end of the season I had 86 wickets in the bag. With Hadlee taking well over 100 and so many batsmen piling up the runs (and much of that form being reproduced in limited-overs games as well) it was disappointing that we finished runners-up in the Championship and the John Player League and could not get past the semi-finals of the Benson and Hedges Cup, which we lost to Lancashire by six wickets. It was easy to say, as mentioned earlier, that Mike Bore's heroic last-gasp efforts denied us the title and a brute of a wicket at Moreton-in-Marsh dearly cost us one Sunday game, but in the end I think it was all down to luck. A couple of breaks did go against us during the summer and they were to prove crucial. We lacked nothing in skill, performance or leadership, but it is a matter of necessity that while there are winners, someone always has to finish second, and in 1984 that was our fate.

We felt it again a year later at Lord's when we lost to Essex on the last ball of the NatWest final and in general the summer of 1985 is one I would like to gloss over and quietly forget. Although our batting remained at a very high standard, Hadlee's penetration with the ball had been dulled by an arduous tour to the West Indies with New Zealand before the season began. I too struggled as time and again we came up against the deadest of pitches. Counties were well aware of our capabilities and went out of their way to negate our strengths. Playing in all but two of our Championship fixtures I slogged my way through 716 overs, but for all the hard work I took only 55 wickets and both the thought of an England recall and more success at Notts at times seemed light years away.

Twelve months on I had exactly the same thoughts, as 1986 turned out to be almost a combination of the previous two years. A unique agreement between Notts and the New Zealand tour management meant that Hadlee would be available to us between his Test and one-day international commitments. It worked out well for all sides since the Kiwis had brought with them to England three young fast bowlers who they were hoping would gain valuable experience playing in their county matches, whereas Hadlee had nothing to prove. He could maintain his cutting edge fighting for honours with us and at the same time work hard within the county on his benefit. We had an added bonus in the return of Rice as a full-time bowler; what he lacked in pace after three years of neck trouble he more than made up for with his experience and as usual there was a stack of runs flowing from the batsmen.

Yet for all my improved haul of 71 wickets, taken despite a prolonged hamstring complaint, we ended up empty-handed again – fourth in the Championship race (we might have finished second had we beaten Northants in our final match), beaten semi-finalists in the Benson and Hedges Trophy and third in the Sunday League. We were by then an experienced and settled side, but all of us knew that Rice and Hadlee were in their mid-thirties and considering retiring from the county scene and it was becoming a question of whether we could actually win something before it was time to start on another team-rebuilding exercise.

The Notts committee spent the early months of the winter persuading Hadlee and Rice to return for one more season, while I was busy preparing for a hectic twenty-second season in first-class cricket knowing that I had to try to fit in a benefit as well. It was a tremendous boost that the club had offered to reward me for my services, but unlike some players approaching their thirty-eighth birthday, retirement was the furthest thing from my mind. And I tried to keep the benefit there too whenever possible, arranging functions only if they did not interfere with my playing schedule.

If anyone had any doubts about whether I would be able to concentrate on cricket with so much happening off the field, I quickly silenced them when Surrey visited Trent Bridge late in April for our opening fixture of the campaign. The Test and County Cricket Board had decided to experiment for one year by leaving wickets uncovered during rain interruptions in the hope that old-fashioned 'sticky dogs' would help produce a new generation of spin bowlers around the counties. It was all very well but I felt that it might leave a wet surface on top of a hard base and didn't fancy facing some of the West Indian quick bowlers around the circuit on drying wickets. That was to happen occasionally during the summer, but for the pipe-opener with Surrey the weather stayed kind and so too was my form as I picked up six wickets in their first innings and then followed up with a fighting 54 in our reply to earn a first-innings lead of 33 and maximum batting points. Unfortunately we were unable to finish the visitors off and it started a pattern that was to frustrate us for several weeks. We began the season with seven successive draws and it was only on the last day of June that we registered our first victory, beating Kent at Canterbury. Although we had made a mess, our Benson and Hedges qualifiers finishing fourth in our group, from that win onwards our season picked up with amazing speed. We reeled off a succession of Sunday League wins and swept aside Suffolk, Middlesex and Derbyshire in the early rounds of the NatWest Trophy. Our confidence was sky-high as we began the second half of the Championship programme.

The computer at Lord's had been kind to us by leaving an unbalanced programme in the final weeks of the season with seven of our last nine matches due to be played at home. Although I was prepared to defend allegations of pitch rigging to the death, we knew that Ron Allsopp would present us with surfaces on which results could be forced. While Hadlee turned the NatWest Trophy final against Northants on its head to give us one title, we all contributed in the Championship as we turned five of those seven home matches into victories, culminating in a victory over Glamorgan who had been our last scalps in the 1981 Championship triumph. Although our programme had ended with us top of the table we still had an agonising wait since Lancashire could still match us. They had to take maximum points from their final match of the season which would be no mean achievement since they were scheduled to face Essex at Chelmsford. In the event they were bowled out for only 220 and while they won the match by 89 runs, the title was already ours. Unfortunately the strain of chasing three titles over the last couple of months took its toll in the Sunday League where we could only finish runners-up.

Much of the praise for our double success was again heaped on Hadlee who failed by only three wickets to complete the double for a second time and it must be said that both he and Rice made it clear that, while it might have been their final season, both were determined to bow out in a big way. After a couple of quiet seasons with the ball and in spite of the benefit, I was bowling back at my best, taking 82 wickets to finish second in the averages. Interestingly enough as I looked at the NatWest Trophy when it was displayed in the members' bar at Trent Bridge, I discovered it was worth £30,000 which was more than my benefit would raise. But it would have been unfair on my teammates, as had been known to happen elsewhere, for me to turn up on the morning of any game legless or even groggy after a benefit function the night before.

The two winner's medals meant more to me than any benefit cheque, but the thing I treasured most was the call that came from the selectors telling me that I was in the tour party for the following winter after so many years of being overlooked by England. I might have been 38, but it was going to be a fresh challenge and although I already had more major domestic honours behind me than some players achieve in their whole careers, I felt a new chapter in my life was about to begin.

The departure of Hadlee and Rice at the end of the season left Notts with a big hole to fill. In the retirement of two men we had lost two seam bowlers and two batsmen capable of winning matches in either department as well as a captain right out of the top bracket. In a bid to replace the irreplaceable the committee signed Franklyn Stephenson as our new overseas player for 1988 and he arrived at Trent Bridge with a fair amount to prove. Our fans might have hoped for, but could not expect, another Hadlee or Rice. Stephenson had spent two years with Gloucestershire in the early 1980s without tearing up stumps, while for the previous four years he had been out of first-class cricket altogether having been banned for life by the West Indies for taking part in two rebel South African tours.

He turned out to be a great success for us in his first season. A friendly character in the dressing room, he did as much as any could have asked to fill the gaps on the field by emulating Hadlee's feat and completing the double.

In fact he gave tremendous value for money in his first year and it was largely due to his efforts, and a magnificent season from Kevin Cooper who also managed 100 wickets, that we finished fifth in the Championship when everyone else was expecting us to sink well down the table.

It was not a happy season for me since I had returned from the England tour to New Zealand with a groin strain after trying to jump a small fence on my way to a practice round. It seemed to clear up quite quickly but early in the season, while in the field at Edgbaston, it went again. I tried to play on with it, but in a damp summer the wet grounds created a problem and I was constantly playing with pain-killing injections.

Off the field, despite our performances, all was not well, though reports of bitter dressing room rows that filtered out were greatly exaggerated. They centred around Robinson who had been given the difficult task of captaining the side on Rice's departure. Superb opening batsman that he is, Robinson is the first to admit that he is not the world's greatest communicator and after years of playing under an extrovert like Rice it was obviously going to take time for all of us to adjust to the change of leadership.

While Robinson and Chris Broad had opened the batting together for several seasons at both county and Test level theirs turned out to be the biggest clash of personalities. Broad is a cricketer who speaks his mind as he had shown when he announced publicly that he was leaving Gloucester-shire because he felt his chance of playing for England would be higher with another county. At Trent Bridge, after Rice's retirement, he was quite open about his ambitions to take over the captaincy and the disharmony between the two reached a head three months into the season.

In July, Worcestershire visited Trent Bridge for a county match and after three low-scoring innings we won the game when Robinson, batting last, scored a quite brilliant 107 not out to lead us to a six-wicket win. But while he should have been able to enjoy the triumph Robinson was so depressed about the dressing-room atmosphere that he went to the committee and resigned. The next day the papers were full of stories that senior players in the side had forced him out of office and my name was put about as one of the leading troublemakers. I was horrified when I was mentioned on television as being at the centre of the trouble. I think people automatically assumed that because I was the senior player, I must have been involved. I was furious and felt that to clear my own name I ought to make a public statement in support of Robinson. I had recognised the problems he was having with the team and along with other players had spoken to Robinson about it, but not in an effort to get him to quit, merely to pass on some good advice. I firmly believed that given time to settle into a difficult job he would make a good captain.

The following season in 1989 the quick progress made by youngster Paul Pollard split the Broad–Robinson opening partnership on a permanent basis and while their profession-alism has never let the captaincy interfere with their work at the crease, both players seemed happier, and even more so in 1990 when Broad made over 2,200 first-class runs and Robinson 1,747. The winning of the Benson and Hedges Cup in 1989 proved that we were not a spent force after the retirement of the two all-rounders and with young talent at the club beginning to mature, a new side was being con-structed to challenge for honours in the 1990s.

7

A LONG HARD WINTER

The tour itinerary worked out for England's players for the winter of 1987–88 was one of the most gruelling ever. After visiting India and Pakistan for the fourth World Cup there were also trips to Pakistan and New Zealand for two series of three tests each. There was some relief in the shape of a two-week break in England with our families at Christmas between visits to Pakistan and New Zealand for two series of three Tests each. Not everyone was scheduled to be involved in the whole programme, the selectors deciding to choose three different squads to cope with the varying conditions.

Although it had been four years since I had last played for England I felt my overall form during the summer with Notts might not go unnoticed having bowled over 800 overs and taken 82 wickets en route to our Championship triumph and produced several important performances as we won the NatWest Trophy. But with such a long gap since I had been part of the England set-up, as the end of the season approached I was making plans to redecorate our home. I certainly did not expect to be involved in the World Cup where, with England limited to taking a small party of fourteen by the competition rules, I felt that John Emburey would go as the only spin bowler. In the event I was one of the hard core of players picked for all three legs of the programme and that meant spending something like 170 nights away from home with the corresponding number of daily hassles with airports and hotels – problems which were always magnified on the sub-continent.

Knowing that I would be celebrating my thirty-ninth birthday somewhere in New Zealand and that such a long tour would demand an exceedingly high level of fitness more suited to a younger player, I could have declined the selectors' invitation to tour – in fact I had a ready-made excuse since 1987 was the year of my benefit at Trent Bridge and by travelling with England I would miss out on three lucrative months of fund raising.

In the event I barely gave that possibility a second thought. Firstly I really fancied the idea of playing in the World Cup. I also wanted to add to my meagre total of Test caps and finally I had always found the benefit system demeaning. Fairly soon after the Notts committee had informed me of their decision to grant a benefit I had spoken to Chris about the way we would approach it and insisted that I would do nothing that would affect my cricket. Many players before and since have virtually ignored their game for twelve months and gone round holding out the begging-bowl to secure a future for themselves and their families after retiring from the game, but that was not for me.

The decision not to spend all my waking hours on fund-raising probably cost the Hemmings household a small fortune. During the season, when Notts were riding the crest of a wave on their way to the double, support and interest from the public was incredible but I ended the year with only £22,750 when other Test players and some who had never played for England were passing the £100,000 mark. Still, it was my decision and at least I could sleep easily. The time has surely come for benefits to be scrapped and for counties to begin operating schemes like the one started up by Essex. There, the county, in conjunction with their benefits and the co-operation of the players, has set up a trust which is fed by funds raised from benefit-style functions. When a player leaves the game, at whatever age, he receives a pay-out from the trust to give him a kick start in the world outside cricket. The system not only caters for the older pro with many years' service but also helps youngsters who perhaps after just a couple of years on the staff have discovered they will not make the grade. The benefit system, on the other hand, only looks after long-serving players and has been used by some counties to blackmail underpaid players into remaining with them even though they might wish to move elsewhere.

Delighted to be back in the England fold for the winter, there was barely time for the champagne bubbles to go flat in the Trent Bridge dressing room before we set off for Delhi and the opening ceremony for the World Cup. It was the start of the most hectic month's cricket of my life since from the Indian capital we had to fly to Pakistan to begin our qualifying games, then move back to India to finish them off with the real prospect of returning to Pakistan for the semi-finals before hopping back to Calcutta for the final.

The whole idea was made worse for me by the amount of flying involved. I am not a happy person on a plane at the best of times but in India and Pakistan, where many of the aircraft look and sound around fifteen years old and appear to be held together by bits of chewing gum, the extra stress does not do wonders for the nervous system. There was also the added tension at airports whenever we flew between Pakistan and India – the two old enemies may have buried the hatchet on the cricket field to wrestle the World Cup away from England but politically they were still at loggerheads and we were put through an endless series of security checks and some body searches before every take-off.

Nevertheless, my enthusiasm for the tasks that lay ahead was boundless even though the signs of a trouble-free trip were not promising. The World Cup opening ceremony in Delhi, featuring a friendly between Pakistan and India, was very poorly attended and a nightmare of tight security owing to the fact that it was attended by the Indian Prime Minister Rajiv Gandhi.

But this was nothing compared to the journey we had to make for the first match – flying up to Lahore and then starting off just after dawn in a procession of coaches escorted by armed police and soldiers for the 80-mile drive to Gujranwala where we were to face the West Indies. With John Emburey the first choice off spinner I was left on the sidelines and much as I wanted to be part of the action, by the end of the game I was glad to have spent the day in the dressing room.

It was one of the hottest I can remember and with the local industrial pollution providing a choking atmosphere it was not surprising that both teams were suffering from exhaustion by the end of play. Given the West Indies' previous record in the World Cup we were very much the underdogs, but after the West Indies had asked us to score 244 we scraped through by two wickets with nine balls to spare thanks to Allan Lamb. He hammered Courtney Walsh for 31 runs in two overs just when we looked like falling well short. Lamb almost passed out when he returned to the dressing room while Walsh, the most experienced member of the West Indies attack, and expected to be the most reliable, had clearly been affected by the heat.

Moving on to Rawalpindi for the second of our qualifying games in Group B against co-hosts Pakistan I was pretty confident of getting my first taste of World Cup action since the wicket was likely to turn and two of our seamers, Gladstone Small and Derek Pringle, had proved pretty expensive in the first match. Rain, however, prevented play on the first day and with water having seeped under the covers we went into the game on the second morning with an unchanged attack. Again our bowling was slightly off the mark and we lost by 18 runs, but the result was clouded by a confrontation between Javed Miandad and our skipper Mike Gatting. Miandad reacted badly after being given out lbw to Phil DeFreitas; it was the first time it had ever happened to him in an international in Pakistan and he was reluctant to leave the crease. To put it politely, Mike suggested Javed should head for the pavilion which he did after making a threatening gesture with his bat. This was just the first incident in a series which later made the tour notorious.

I finally got my big chance in the third game against Sri Lanka played at Peshawar, the frontier town in north-west Pakistan. Although the bowling of Small and Pringle was still giving the tour selectors much food for thought it was actually a knee injury to Neil Foster that presented me with an opening and our batsmen made it a pretty easy baptism. Half-centuries from Gatting, Gooch and Lamb allowed us to pile up 296 for 4 – a pretty useful total since our defeat against Pakistan meant we might need a high run-rate later to qualify for the semi-finals. But we had one major headache: with heavy clouds threatening a wash-out we had to bowl at least 25 overs to make the result stand. To get through our overs quickly Gatting introduced Emburey and me to the attack with their innings only nine overs old and while the rain never materialised despite leaden skies, together we put the results beyond doubt. The Sri Lankans had subsided quickly to 37 for 3 and John kept them in a stranglehold conceding just 26 runs in his ten overs while mine cost only 31. Along the way I picked up the wickets of Ranjan Madugalle and Aravinda De Silva and felt that I had done well enough to keep my place as we moved on to Karachi for our second game against Pakistan.

It was not the happiest of trips, for while Gatting and Bill Athey made sure our final total of 247 was respectable with a fourth-wicket stand of 135, we did not bowl well enough to contain Pakistan. While I only went for four runs an over, Small had another nightmare conceding 63 runs in his nine overs and we flew back to India knowing that we had to beat the West Indies a second time in Jaipur to qualify for the semi-finals. It was always going to be a tough task

73

since the West Indies would not only be seeking revenge for Gujranwala but also had to win themselves to stay in the competition.

Given the natural stroke-playing ability of most Caribbean batsmen Mike Gatting and Micky Stewart took a courageous decision to stick with an attacking formula that included both Emburey and me, but our chances of a victory once Viv Richards put us into bat were going to depend heavily on the batsman coping first with the West Indies pace attack. It was Graham Gooch who accomplished that task with a marvellous and disciplined innings for 92. He started off at a canter and we had 151 on the board after only 30 overs and while the middle order batting fell away slightly he hung around to make sure we reached 269 and an upset was very much on the cards.

In one-day games I had always preferred to bowl second, though it helps to have a good total to defend, and we certainly had that at Jaipur. It looked even more impressive as Phil DeFreitas had Desmond Haynes caught early on by Bill Athey and Emburey at the start of his spell dismissed the very dangerous Phil Simmons. But all that good work began to count for nothing once Richards and Richie Richardson began to take us apart with a stand of 82. Viv always looks to dominate bowlers and on this occasion I was his target as he swept me for two successive sixes, though the second one, which came off the top edge, only just dropped over the head of DeFreitas standing on the long-leg boundary. Given that Jaipur had such a small outfield I am sure that on 99 per cent of international grounds that shot would have dropped comfortably into the fielder's hands.

As the stand grew so did the confidence of the two batsmen with Viv making room on the back foot to smash me past cover for four, but he tried it once too often, was bowled and suddenly we were back in the match. I had a field day. By the time we had posted a 34-run victory I had helped dismiss Gus Logie with a catch at backward-square-leg, run out Roger Harper with a direct throw at the stumps and bowled Courtney Walsh. I may have been 38 but I had proven in the heat that I was as fit and able to dash about as any other player in the side.

We were all in a buoyant mood as we left Jaipur and able to make light of another tortuous journey involving an overnight stop in Bombay en route for our final qualifying game against Sri Lanka at Pune. Although we had still not fully guaranteed our place in the semi-finals there seemed little doubt we would go through. We could even afford to lose to Sri Lanka provided the West Indies did not beat Pakistan by a huge run rate which was highly unlikely. In the event the equation did not come into play. I picked up three more wickets as we restricted the Sri Lankans to 218 and Graham Gooch did the rest, picking up his second successive man-of-the-match award as we romped home by eight wickets with as many overs to spare. Crucially, by finishing runners-up to Pakistan in the group, we had avoided the need to return to Lahore for our semi-final and instead faced a short trip to Bombay to face the host nation India.

It meant we had an extra day to prepare ourselves and at the last minute it was decided that we should make the journey down from Pune by train rather than air. That came as a refreshing change as much as a relief. In general I had become bored with life off the cricket field on the sub-continent. Television in both India and Pakistan is generally not worth watching with many of the programmes in a foreign language and even in the few hotels that showed in-house movies they were sometimes so heavily censored on the strict local moral grounds that themes were lost along the way. In Pakistan, again because of the Moslem laws, there were no bars in the hotels, decent restaurants were few and far between and room service was a lottery – the food sometimes didn't arrive, when it did it was invariably cold and hours late and more often than not it contained different dishes from the ones that had been ordered.

The train journey, however, gave me a chance to forget all those frustrations and just to sit back and enjoy the breathtaking scenery as the train ambled along the Deccan plateau and down through the foothills towards the coast. It provided my fondest memory of the sub-continent and put me in the right frame of mind for the big game which lay ahead.

Ever since Pakistan and India had outbid England for the right to stage the World Cup, the two host nations had been praying their sides would reach the final and there was more than an element of suspicion that the draw for the two qualifying zones had been manœuvred to keep them apart until the last possible moment. But with such a deep passion for the game in that part of the world we knew all the pressure would be on us and the venue was not going to help.

Bombay's Wankhede Stadium, the city's third and newest Test ground, is a large concrete bowl with stands that climb up steeply from right by the boundary's edge and when full with a 50,000 plus crowd – though I swear there were probably over 60,000 jammed in for the semi-final – it seems that every spectator is breathing down your neck. The noise too is incredible as it reverberates around under the roof with no room to escape and every now and then it is punctuated by a series of deafening bangs from a string of fire-crackers. For the Indians almost any game of cricket is a festival and a World Cup semi-final proved even more so, especially since the Indians had stunned the cricketing fraternity by winning the 1983 World Cup and looked on course for a second triumph after winning all but one of their six qualifying games.

On the other hand we had Graham Gooch in marvellous form. It was somewhat ironic that the dullness of the cricket on Keith Fletcher's Indian tour in the winter of 1981–82 had so depressed Gooch that it was a major influence in him joining, and later captaining, the first of the unofficial tours to South Africa. Having served his three-year international suspension he found himself back in India for the first time and was clearly out to dispel those bad memories. Kapil Dev asked us to bat first hoping the ball would seam around on a damp pitch but Gooch, on his way to yet another man-of-the-match award, and Gatting doomed that scheme to failure in a 117-run third-wicket stand and with 254 runs in the bank the final was beckoning us.

But we only booked the ticket for Calcutta as the direct result of a stand-up disagreement between Gatting and me which hardly went unnoticed in the middle of the pitch. I had been brought into the attack after DeFreitas and Neil Foster had made the early breakthroughs dismissing Krish Srikkanth and Sunil Gavaskar, who bowed out of international cricket after a tremendous career leaving his off-stump lying on the ground.

Instead of keeping on the pressure as I had done in the previous game suddenly I was carted all over the place by Mohammad Azharuddin and Chetan Pandit. Twenty-seven runs came off my first three overs and despite having words with the skipper he refused my request for a man to be posted on the mid-wicket boundary. Instead Gatting took me off and used Gooch's gentle medium pace to fill the gap. It was only when Kapil began to put India right back in the driving seat with a 22-ball blitz that yielded 26 runs that I was brought back into attack.

Immediately Kapil smashed me for another four over Gatting's head at square-leg and it was only after yet another exchange of views that he reluctantly agreed to retreat back to the ropes. My insistence that he move could hardly have been justified any quicker as the very next ball Kapil, to the disgust of a stunned Indian crowd, attempted to repeat the shot and Gatting held on to a catch that turned the course of the match. From being the villain of the English attack

77

after my first spell, suddenly I was the hero and in the next five overs I cleared up the Indian innings single-handed. I trapped Azharuddin lbw for 64 and later finished off the innings by having Chetan Sharma caught by Allan Lamb and Ravi Shastri, going for a bit hit, caught behind with successive balls. We had won by 35 runs to join Australia in the final. They had beaten Pakistan in Lahore the previous day to shatter the plans of the World Cup organisers who had hoped for a final featuring the two host nations.

While the Australians had vast experience of one-day cricket, given the explosion of the shortened game Down Under in the years after Kerry Packer, we had no reason to feel anything but confident as we flew to Calcutta for the final which was to be played in front of an 80,000 crowd at Eden Garden, which had been partially rebuilt and tidied up to make a magnificent setting for the climax of the competition.

Although in the end we only lost the match by seven runs we virtually handed the game to the Aussies on a plate in the first hour of the game as both DeFreitas and Small seemed overcome by a sense of the big occasion, lost all direction and allowed Geoff Marsh and David Boon to put on 52 in the first ten overs. There is nothing quite as confident as an Australian team when it's on top and even though Emburey and I tried to plug the gaps in the middle of their innings it was too late.

After an early setback when we lost Tim Robinson, Bill Athey played an anchor role with 58 that allowed us to get back on target to score 254 which would have been the highest winning score by a side batting second in the competition. But two rushes of blood cost us our chance of glory. Athey was run out attempting a suicidal third run to Steve Waugh and then Gatting played a disastrous reverse-sweep to the first ball bowled by Allan Border – it was an awful shot and only Gatting knows why he tried to attempt it.

Losing the final was a bitter disappointment after the

stirring earlier wins over the all-powerful West Indies and the upset we caused when we beat India in Bombay. Along with most of the cricketing world I for one had not expected us to do so well in the competition, but having overcome so many obstacles, to fall at the final fence was a sad anticlimax and the England plane was full of saddened hearts as we flew to Pakistan to begin the second leg of the winter programme.

After a practice match in Pakistan we confirmed our limited-overs form by beating our hosts in the one-day international series 3–0, Gooch playing magnificently to score 142 in the second game at Karachi and following up with a further 57 in Peshawar. The early games were particularly important for the new members of the squad who had flown out to increase the size of our party after the World Cup. Among them was Nick Cook and I was more than slightly peeved when he walked straight into the side at my expense for the first Test in Lahore. Throughout the World Cup John Emburey and I had both bowled consistently well, and I certainly thought I had done enough to win my first Test cap for four years. I had even taken four wickets in our opening warm-up game against the President's XI at Rawalpindi and it was more frustrating to know I wouldn't be bowling on a wicket in the Qaddafi Stadium which looked certain to turn after being used twice for World Cup matches.

The Pakistani side went in with three spinners leaving only one specialist seamer, Wasim Akram, and medium-paced all-rounder Mudassar Nazar to share the new ball. As we lost by an innings and 87 runs Akram and Mudassar bowled only 22 overs between them in the game, confirming my view that I should have been in the England side. But any personal feelings were completely overshadowed by a series of questionable umpiring decisions that went against us. In our second innings Chris Broad made a stand which drew widespread criticism by staying at the crease for around half a minute when umpire Shakeel Khan gave him out caught at the wicket by Ashraf Ali off the bowling of Iqbal Qasim. Although there is no point in arguing once an umpire has raised his finger, Peter Lush, our tour manager, summed up the feelings of all the players later when he told the press that he felt Broad's action was the culmination of frustrations which had built up inside the team over the previous three days.

We had little chance of lifting our spirits when we travelled up-country for another practice match against the Punjab Chief Minister's XI at Sahiwal. Some lucky players, including skipper Mike Gatting, were allowed to stay behind in Lahore and to rest in the luxury of one of the city's top hotels while those of us involved in the game were accommodated in the rest rooms of a local biscuit factory. I know that some touring teams in England occasionally find themselves playing at an outpost away from the main cricketing centres with only a fairly basic hotel in which to stay at nights, but at least there is normally a restaurant or a pub nearby to make the evening more passable. In provincial towns on the sub-continent in both Pakistan and India there is simply no equivalent and I question whether touring teams should have to visit such places in this day and age. It is certainly hard to play six hours of cricket in burning sunshine after a sleepless night in an uncomfortable and not necessarily clean bed with no promise of a proper evening meal to follow.

At least when we got to Faisalabad for the second Test I had the consolation of being picked as the selectors decided to follow the Pakistan approach and take three spinners into the game. But any cricket was to be overshadowed by the now infamous clash between Gatting and umpire Shakoor Rana just as play was coming to a close on the second day. Hundreds of thousands of words have been written about that incident both on the day and in the years since, but while Gatting has been criticised from pillar to post, have people ever bothered to analyse exactly what led to our captain getting involved in a shouting match out in the middle with an umpire? Since it was I who actually sparked the whole thing off I think I am as qualified as any to put it into a true perspective.

After our defeat in Lahore, and with another Test wicket that had been purpose-built to suit Abdul Qadir and his fellow Pakistani spinners, we did exceptionally well after Gatting won the toss to score 292 with Chris Broad grinding out 116 in a shade over seven hours to form the backbone of the innings. We knew it was going to be a hard task to get back into the series after losing that opening game but we fought like tigers in the field on that second afternoon.

Neil Foster had worked wonders with the new ball to have Mudassar and Ramiz Raja caught off the edge and John Emburey had raised our hopes with the wickets of Javed Miandad, Ijaz Ahmed and Shoaib Mohammad. With stumps approaching I was rushing through an over to Salim Malik, desperately trying to stop him getting a single so that we could have one more over at Aamer Malik, the new batsman at the other end.

It was my idea that David Capel, who had been fielding on the long-leg boundary, should be moved up to save the single should Salim attempt to turn me away on the on side. He was standing in his crease looking at me as I shouted to Gatting, fielding at short-leg, to move him. It is now history that Shakoor accused Gatting of cheating by waving with his hand to Capel to hurry and move into position just as I was about to bowl. He claimed that Gatting was moving a fielder without the batsman's knowledge, yet seconds earlier Salim had acknowledged my request for Capel to be moved. The words that were exchanged out in the middle are unprintable in a book meant for family consumption but once everyone had cooled down and play resumed we only had time for me to complete the over and an opportunity of getting a sixth wicket to increase our advantage in the match had been lost.

The whole incident seemed suspicious from the start and when the next morning Shakoor refused to restart play until he got an apology from Gatting, there were other factors which confirmed my fears that we were going to be stopped from winning that Test whatever the cost. Lush drove for hours to try to find the Pakistan Board secretary to get the matter resolved as quickly as possible, but he was not available for a meeting at a time when the whole question of cricketing relations between the two countries was at risk. In the end Gatting sent Shakoor the written apology he demanded but it was a travesty for our captain – I and Mike *had* informed Salim that the fielder was to be moved, Gatting had *not* cheated or even started the row and yet he had to apologise. With the loss of over a day's play we had to settle for a draw.

We lost the series 1–0 when the third Test too ended in stalemate. I didn't play in the game, but apart from the fact that I had always wanted to play as many Tests as possible it was no great loss. When Raman Subba Row, the Chairman of the Test and County Cricket Board, and Alan Smith, the Chief Executive, flew out to Karachi to try to defuse what was growing into a major political incident, I was all for flying home with the rest of the team and against playing the final Test. It was only when Gatting came back from a private meeting with Subba Row and Smith that we showed solidarity with our captain's decision to stay on and play.

The Christmas break back at home with our families was an ideal opportunity for us to try to forget the bitterness of Pakistan and recharge our batteries for the New Year visit to New Zealand which was to be interrupted briefly while we popped into Australia to play a one-day international and a Test match as part of the country's huge Bicentenary celebrations. It was a pity that we didn't have more spare time in Australia to enjoy the many events that had been laid on but at least the pilot of our jumbo jet made sure we didn't miss out on one spectacular sight as we flew to Sydney on Australia Day.

Our arrival coincided with the end of a month's long voyage for a fleet of old tall ships which had sailed from England to re-enact the original discovery of the continent and while they were gathered with hundreds of other small craft the pilot did a double low-level pass over Sydney harbour so that we were given a great aerial view of the boats from the windows of the plane.

With so much happening in Sydney at the time, the Test match between cricket's two oldest foes attracted less attention than usual – a pity because we so nearly pulled off a victory to spoil the Australian party. The crowd on the first day wasn't too bad but once Broad had put us in command with 139 – his fourth century in only six Tests Down Under – it was clear that Australia would struggle to save the game. After all the traumas of Pakistan I relished the chance to play in such a big game and we bowled them out for 214 to earn a first-innings lead of 211. I chipped in with three wickets. There were just over five sessions remaining when Australia batted for a second time but our chances of bowling them out were severely reduced since both our leading strike bowlers, Graham Dilley and Neil Foster, left the field with injuries. With only the ever-eager David Capel in support that left Emburey and me with a mammoth task. Unfortunately the Sydney wicket, which had so often helped spinners, became slower and less co-operative by the hour and even though we bowled 90 overs between us we could not uproot David Boon. The Australian opener made a defiant 184 and remained unbeaten at the end when the Aussies, having lost only two wickets, secured the draw.

The Bicentenary Test was the highlight of what turned out to be a very tedious tour for me, since I was left on the sidelines for the first two drawn Tests in New Zealand and when I finally got a taste of the action in Wellington it was on a shirt-front of a wicket. That game too was heading nowhere in particular as the Kiwis scored 512 for 6 declared and there had been no calamities in our reply when torrential rain washed out the final two days. As if we had not played enough one-day games that winter the programme ended with four one-day internationals but since I was not picked for any of them I couldn't wait to get home. Although it was great, at the age of 39, to have been back on the England scene again it had been a long hard winter and with John Emburey still rated by the England management as the leading off-spinner, I was no closer to being established as an England regular.

8

ONE-DAY MAGIC

The triumphs that I enjoyed in the 1987 World Cup made me chuckle on the quiet and I doubt whether Richard Hadlee realised that I was laughing at this great man's expense. Occasionally my mind would fly back to pre-season team talks we had had at the start of one season in the early 1980s with the zonal rounds of the Benson and Hedges Cup about to be played.

Notts' record in the previous couple of years in the competition had been pretty dismal and Clive Rice, anxious to bring about some improvement, decided that all the players should get together in the dressing room to work out a strategy for the new campaign. The batsmen had their say and great stress was put on running between wickets while there was the basic normal agreement that alert fielding could make or break any team. Then we started to discuss the bowling tactics. It was still a commonly held view around the counties that accurate medium-pacers held the key to success in any one-day competition, though other critics claimed that it had stunted the development of many a young fast bowler. When it was suggested that I might be able to play a part, Hadlee looked at me from the other side of the room and said very matter-of-factly, 'He cannot bowl in limited-overs games.' And such was the all-rounders' dressing-room influence that the captain made a note and I was duly left out of the opening games. We didn't fare too well that season but for a spinner who it was said couldn't bowl, my performances later in the 1980s, especially for England in one-day internationals, certainly made nonsense of that assertion.

But my one-day memories stretch back much further than Hadlee's comment even though as the years have passed I have rather tried to forget the events of my first-ever visit to Lord's for the big match. The occasion was the 1968 Gillette Cup final when Warwickshire met Sussex who, under Ted Dexter, had been the first county to grasp the tactical ideas that led to trophies on sideboards.

Having had such an explosive Championship debut against Hampshire that summer and played three other first-class matches, I was by then recognised as a first team contender whenever one of our senior players went down with an injury. That was exactly what happened to Tom Cartwright and Jack Bannister as the final approached and having been put on standby for several matches earlier in the competition, I was thrilled to be named in the thirteen for the trip to London. Given my lack of experience the committee eventually decided that Dennis Amiss should be the fifth bowler and while his 12 overs cost 63 runs he scored an unbeaten 44 in a seventh-wicket stand of 60 with AC Smith which pulled us back from the brink of defeat to take the Gillette Cup with three overs to spare.

Just being part of the winning dressing room was a fantastic experience for an eighteen-year-old youngster and I must have got carried away by the victory champagne . . . later that night somewhere in the West End with Mum, Dad and Chris it finally got to me and I collapsed in a heap on the pavement. I remember Chris standing over me saying in a very stern voice, 'Really Eddie, you are embarrassing your parents', but I was beyond caring.

I was still bowling my medium pace in those days and it was long after my conversion to off spin that my role in one-day cricket took on some importance. However, I do think counties are still narrow-minded in the way they

Looking cool (**right**) before my Warwickshire debut against Scotland in 1966, but it was a long hard fight to replace the experience of Lance Gibbs (**below left**) and Tom Cartwright (**below right**)

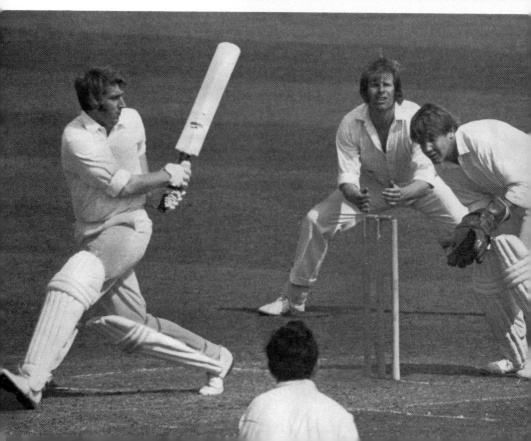

Landmarks with Warwickshire
. . . bowling during my seven
for 40 against Oxford in 1975
and on my way to 80, then my
highest first-class score, against
Worcestershire in 1971

Opposite: Bob Willis and I did
not always see eye to eye, but
he was quick to congratulate
me on my first Test wicket
after I bowled Javed Miandad
in 1982

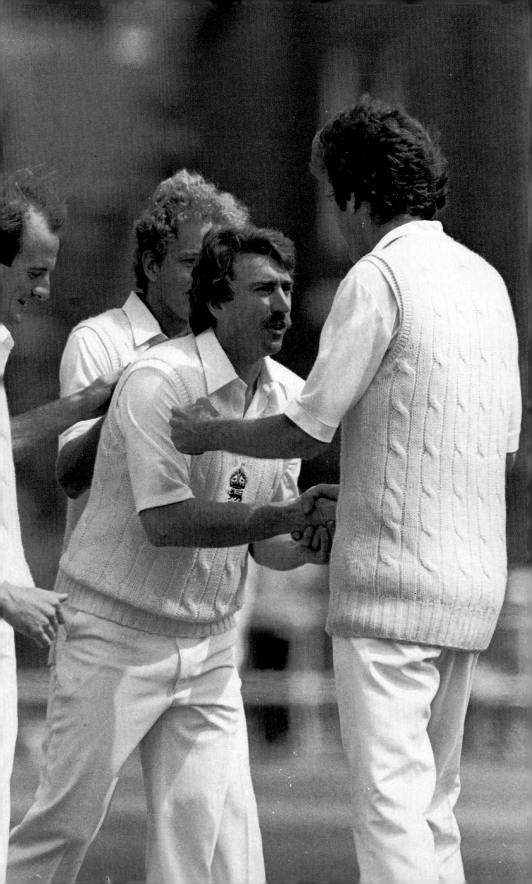

BATSMEN	OUT	F OF W
COOK	2	
TAVARE	16	5
GOWER	24	10
LAMB	29	15
HEMMINGS	95	19
RANDALL	44	26
BOTHAM	32	26
ATTENDANCE	15	19
SUNDRIES	22	

IS PROHIBIT

*ruce, if we let Hemmings score 60 so he was
tired to bowl—how is it he's got 2 for 19?"*

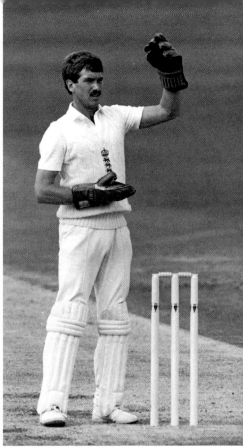

Opposite: England's secret weapon Down
Under in 1982–83 (above left) and my
favourite view of the old scoreboard at
the Sydney Cricket Ground (above right).
Working the ball to leg (below) during
my nightwatchman's innings of 95 in the
fifth Test

Allied at Notts . . . Bruce French (above),
the best gloveman in the business and not
so bad at ordering his end of the day pint.
Basher Hassan, in the side as a batsman,
but worth fifteen to twenty wickets a
season to me with his incredible fielding
at short leg

Above left: Pride is written all over the face of Clive Rice as he lifts the NatWest Trophy in 1987

Above right: Derek Randall – a genius when batting at his best, but such a frustrating character to have on your side

Opposite: All smiles . . . Chris Broad, Tim Robinson and myself as we learn of selection for the 1987 World Cup and jubilation in the English camp as my late burst seals the semi-final victory over India

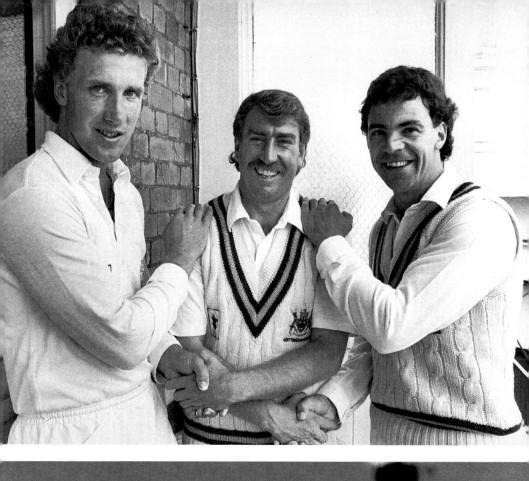

Every picture tells a story ... John Lever wanted the ground to open up and swallow him after I had scored the winning boundary off the last ball in the 1989 Benson and Hedges Cup Final. (**Below**) Notts fans mobbed myself and Bruce French on the way back to the pavilion

Above: Even the boys help out with my tough training schedule

Left: A study in concentration – skipper Graham Gooch and myself during the match against Jamaica at Sabina Park

Opposite: The Coming of Age as I destroy the Kiwis at Edgbaston in 1990. (**Above**) Mike Atherton at slip brilliantly catches Sir Richard Hadlee, but (**below**) has an easier time seeing off Mark Greatbatch

(**Above**) Alec Stewart picks up Ian Rutherford at short leg and by the time we move on to play India at Old Trafford (**below**) Graham Gooch has given me the close field that is a spinner's dream

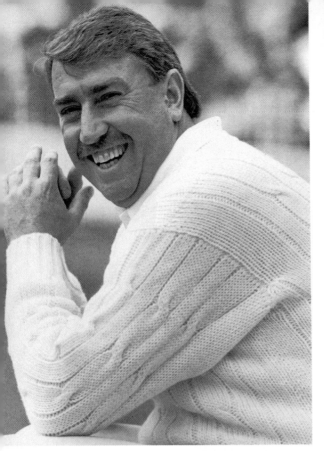

And that's the way
cricket should always be
played . . . with a smile

regard young spinners and one-day cricket. If a youngster is going to make his way through to the top flight he has to be able to maintain his control under pressure – a spinner is of very little use to his captain if he is likely to wilt under a murderous assault in any standard of cricket and there could not be a better place to learn to accept flak and fight back than in the heat of a one-day game when the batsmen are going all out to score runs.

With slow bowling, control is very much a matter of confidence in the mind and over many years I have developed my own strategy for coping with the strains of limited-overs cricket. It is based on the simple premise that if I can bowl to set fields to stop batsmen scoring boundaries then at least half the battle is won. Once they start to try to hit the ball over the top, their room for manoeuvre is considerably less and the risk element considerably greater. But having taken that as my basic strategy I have developed the idea a bit further to the extent that I am actually prepared to give the batsmen the odd single deliberately in a one-day game if in the long run it cuts down their temptation to be a bit more adventurous.

I think most captains would generally be very happy to accept a bowler who in an eight-over spell on a Sunday, or eleven overs in a Benson and Hedges game, gives away less than 3 runs an over. Since taking wickets is not the main priority, a bowler who can prevent the opposition batsmen running wild has done his job. But such restrictions cannot be adhered to if a batsman starts hitting boundaries and if that happens it should only be for one of two reasons – either I have done the unforgivable and bowled a bad ball that deserves punishing or it is near the end of the innings when risks have to be taken.

Outside of those two situations it is actually possible to hoodwink cunningly any batsman out of going for his shots and that is where giving away the odd single with a half-volley (easily pushed for instance down to the man stationed out at deep-long-on) comes into play. If the batsmen can calmly pick up two or three singles an over that way they will see the scoreboard ticking over regularly and begin to think they are doing their job without resorting to the sort of slog that could yield a boundary. The fact is that playing in such a manner they can be restricted to a total of say 140 on a Sunday or under 200 in a 55-over contest, which is rarely sufficient. Since the ploy works quite often, at the end of my spell on a Sunday I can look at figures of somewhere around 8–0–23–0 and happily retire to the outfield in the knowledge of a job well done.

That in a nutshell is the Eddie Hemmings theory on how to be a success as a slow bowler in one-day cricket. It got me back my England place in 1987 and kept me in the team in the years that followed. Of course the higher the level of one-day cricket I have played in over the years, the easier it has become to accept pressure-cooker situations, and during the 1980s with Notts I got lots of practice at the top because we were involved in three of the most dramatic finals ever seen at Lord's.

They began with the 1985 NatWest Trophy where we had a dress rehearsal for a tight climax by only beating Worcestershire in the final over of a tense semi-final at New Road – Tim Robinson setting up the victory with a brilliant 139 but then causing the odd nerve to tingle when he was run out in the penultimate over with six runs still wanted.

The final was even more dramatic. On a Lord's pitch ideal for high-scoring contest our bowlers, myself included, were taken apart as Graham Gooch and Brian Hardie cruised through a record opening partnership of 202. Essex's final total of 280 for 2 presented a daunting proposition but we had our own great start as Broad and Robinson responded with a stand of 143. Unfortunately we then lost a series of batsmen who were out trying to keep up a hectic pace and when the last three overs began we were still 37 short of our target.

Derek Randall, however, launched a solo attack on Derek Pringle taking sixteen from the first five deliveries of the final over and so he was left needing two runs off the final ball. Some of us in the dressing room could not bear to watch as Randall tried to pull the final delivery away on the leg side only to be caught by Paul Prichard at short mid-wicket. Another inch or two higher and the ball would have cleared him and run up to the grandstand to give us victory.

Although that great fight-back finished in disappointment, two years later when we returned to Lord's to face Northants we managed to dig ourselves out from an even deeper hole and set up the first leg of our 1987 double.

Heavy overnight rain meant that another capacity Lord's crowd had to wait until 11.45 am for a start and in trying to get the match completed inside one day the umpires reduced the game to 50 overs. We asked Northants to bat and although Richard Hadlee and Andy Pick both bowled well at the start they could not prevent Geoff Cook and Wayne Larkins putting on 61 for the first wicket which was to prove a solid base for the batsmen who followed. Clive Rice bowled me from the Nursery End and I just couldn't settle – conceding 52 runs from my ten overs was well in excess of my normal game-plan and Northants eventually managed 228 for 3.

It was not quite the size of total Northants had at one time threatened to compile but it was still big enough and began to look massive when we set out in search of victory. By the time rain returned to call a halt at 7.10 pm we had subsided to 57 for 4. Winston Davis had taken out both our openers in a devastating opening blast and then we lost two wickets in strange fashion. Paul Johnson somehow got his legs in a complete tangle and fell lbw to Alan Walker and then Randall was bowled by a ball from Nick Cook which was flighted out of the dying sun but was in shadows by the time it reached the batsman.

Our spirits were low as we trudged back up to Trent

Bridge at the end of play to prepare for a Sunday League match against Essex and even that failed to divert our minds from the final because heavy rain meant there was not a ball bowled in the match.

Clive Rice was in a philosophical mood when we assembled back at Lord's on the Monday. To a man the members of the daily press had written off our chances, but Rice still believed we could win if we followed his simple instructions to keep pushing the singles, keep wickets intact and wait for the wayward overs that might eventually come our way. He also knew that with David Capel carrying an injury there was every chance Northants might not be able to continue attacking with their front-line bowlers.

With their retirements from county cricket barely a fort-night away we all knew that both Rice and Richard Hadlee would like to grace their last appearances at headquarters with significant contributions. With his tactics worked out Rice set about proving that his words could be put into practice – boundaries in any event were going to be hard to come by since the weekend rain had left the Lord's outfield sodden. With John Birch providing staunch support the early overs after the resumption were countered without alarms. But then Birch forgot his instructions, played horribly across the line to a ball from Walker and was bowled.

Rice and Hadlee began to swing the match in our direction with a sensible partnership of 62 in fourteen overs, but when the skipper was out in the 42nd over for 63 Hadlee decided to take the game by the scruff of the neck. No one should ever underestimate the part played by Bruce French who was quite magnificent scoring 35, but it was one of Hadlee's greatest innings that saw us lift the trophy.

He needed some luck for in one over from spinner Richard Williams, a huge hit down towards the Mound Stand was carried over the ropes for six by Allan Lamb, Rob Bailey dropped a skier that came out of the sun and Lamb was very close to completing another stinging catch that reached him at ankle height. Eight runs were wanted off the last over and with Hadlee in full cry it shouldn't have been that much of a problem as it was to be bowled by Capel who was still not fully fit.

I was beginning to think I could unbuckle my pads in the dressing room but from the first ball French was unluckily run out when his push for a single was deflected off Hadlee's boot straight to Capel. Still as I walked to the wicket I knew I would be the non-striker in our final push for glory and two strokes from Hadlee's bat completed our fight-back. The first soared over long-off for six and the next was pulled fiercely to the mid-wicket boundary. I had been there at the death to witness Hadlee's last great effort for Notts, but two years later I was to be at centre stage when we once again served up a thrilling finish for our fans.

While not wishing to seem immodest I was quite happy with my own contribution from the very start of our 1989 Benson and Hedges Cup campaign. The draw for the qualifying groups had been kind to us since our first-class opponents Derbyshire, Yorkshire and Somerset were not high up among the bookmakers' favourites. Providing we did not make a complete hash-up we could confidently expect to beat the Minor Counties.

But things did not go smoothly right from the start. Against Derbyshire and the Minor Counties, chasing straightforward targets in the 170s, we lost early wickets in each game only to be rescued in identical fashion as Stephenson and Randall both scored middle-order half-centuries to win the matches. Yorkshire had won the Cup against the odds a year earlier but it had not proved to be a start of a new golden era for the county and we were embarrassed to score only 144 batting first. Their fortunes, however, were so low that they could not take advantage and with Kevin Cooper taking 4 for 9 we won by 33 runs. By the time we travelled to Taunton for the final game we had already qualified for the quarter-finals, though we needed to win to make sure of a home tie. But we came up against the prolific South African Jimmy Cook who made mincemeat of a target of 203 by scoring 79 to give their innings a sound basis. Still, in each game I had bowled my full allocation of eleven overs, only picking up five wickets but conceding a miserly 2.4 runs an over on average.

The draw sent us back to the West Country for a clash with Gloucestershire. Here, a thrilling tie provided me with an experience completely new to me after twenty years of playing one-day cricket at both county and international level and not one that I was in too much of a hurry to repeat afterwards. I had always admired the way John Emburey was prepared to bowl 'at the death' and normally to good effect in limited overs games for England, but I had never been called upon to do the same and frankly never fancied the thought of being slogged all over the place by batsmen who have reached a stage beyond caring whether they lose their wickets or not.

But Tim Robinson was forced to reshuffle all his bowling tactics soon after Gloucestershire set off in search of 223 to win when Stephenson broke down with a bad thigh strain half-way through his fourth over. The days when Notts could always afford to carry a spare, sixth, bowler into games to cover for such emergencies had disappeared with the retirement of the all-rounders Hadlee and Rice, and Robinson had to turn to Chris Broad, whose career record of medium-pace bowling consisted of 16 first-class wickets at the none-too-promising average of 64 runs apiece. Fortunately for us, Broad, playing against the county he had left six years earlier amid some acrimony, was in no mood to be generous to his old employers. He had already taken 106 off them in our innings, was later to pick up two good catches, and his bowling proved to be useful as well.

In nine and a half very respectable overs he conceded only 26 runs and provided the added bonus of taking Paul Romaine's wicket. The disruption however meant that when

Gloucestershire began a tense final over with only seven runs required and two wickets in hand it was up to me to bowl it. Jack Russell scampered two off the first ball, but then went for a big hit only to find Broad's safe hands waiting in the deep at long-off. Next ball David Lawrence also tried to hit me out of the ground, but missed a straight one and while, much to my relief, we were through to a semi-final date with Kent, I was hoping that it was going to be a one-off experience. In many one-day games my final figures of 4 for 47 combined with the exciting finish might just have won me the man-of-the-match award but on that occasion no one could touch Broad's credentials.

We must have had friends in very high places in 1989 as the draw for the semi-finals, which paired us with Kent, meant we had avoided meeting the hot favourites Essex and also Somerset who had beaten us earlier in the competition. Kent, however, served notice that they did not intend to be pushovers in the last three days running up to the match. By strange coincidence we were involved in a Championship fixture at Trent Bridge immediately before the semi-final and while Kent were languishing near the bottom of the table they recorded only their fourth victory that season beating us by four wickets.

Furthermore they achieved an astonishing win after Robinson had set them a stiff target of 311 in their second innings. Despite that batting display we had every reason to be confident from the moment Broad and Paul Pollard had thrilled a packed Trent Bridge crowd with an opening partnership of 141. Our final total of 296 was going to need a competition record score by a side batting second, and while we were hampered by the absence of the still-injured Stephenson, our left-arm spinner Andy Afford ensured a 69-run victory by taking the wickets of Mark Benson, Neil Taylor, Roy Pienaar and Chris Cowdrey in the space of 22 balls. In the other semi-final at Taunton Essex scraped through by four runs so the stage was set for a repeat of the 1985 NatWest Trophy final.

Memories of Randall falling to the last-ball catch were still clear in most of our minds and we desperately wanted revenge, though my immediate thoughts as the game approached centred around a niggling injury that left me touch and go to make the start.

I had picked up a groin strain the previous week and was in extreme discomfort when we went out to practise before the game. Left to my own devices I don't think I would have played though I knew pain-killing injections could be pretty effective. But the decision was taken out of my hands when Robinson came up to me in the dressing room and said that however bad I felt the county selectors had decided I should play, even though there was a risk that I would break down and since the injury had happened before the match we wouldn't be allowed a substitute fielder.

A different competition maybe but the final turned out to be almost a carbon copy of the one four years earlier with Essex batting first. Stephenson's famous 'windmill ball' – a slow-looping off spinner bowled off his full run – created some early mirth for the sun-baked crowd as it completely deceived Brian Hardie, but Graham Gooch with 48 and Alan Lilley with a brave 95 not out, which held together the Essex middle order, allowed them to reach 243 for 7 off their 55 overs. Given the small boundaries at Lord's and the overall strength of the opposition I was not too happy with my own bowling although conceding 47 runs from eleven overs still meant that in three appearances at Lord's in a final I had not bowled at my very best.

Our reply, which was later to be labelled 'the battle of cricket's grandads', got off to a disastrous start as John Lever, aged 40 like me but four days younger, proved that age and a stomach operation had not dulled the powers which had once made him a fine bowler at Test level. Lever had us in immediate trouble as he dismissed both Pollard and Broad in his first five-over spell.

I have always been full of admiration for Tim Robinson when he is in full flow at the crease and he can rarely have played a better innings than his captain's knock of 86 which, along with Paul Johnson's quick-fire 54, pulled us back into the game. The skipper could have won the game for us off his own bat but Derek Randall, a nervous character in everyday life, was at his fidgety worst when he called Robinson for an impossible single which had no chance against a high-class fielder like John Stephenson. Fortunately Kevin Evans, a young all-rounder, helped steady our innings but Randall was proving to be a nightmare for our team. People who do not know Randall often describe him as a complex character. In fact he is just the opposite, but there is no other cricketer that I have played with or against that has managed to infuriate me more – at times I have just wanted to tear my hair out.

Arkle has more natural ability in his little finger than many cricketers have in their whole body as he proved with the magnificent 174 he scored for England under enormous pressure in the 1976 Centenary Test at Melbourne. In full flow with his exceptional timing as a batsman or as an agile fielder he is one of the finest players I have seen, yet for all the tons of ability he has barely an ounce of self-confidence. And what he had drained out of him when we were on tour with England in the winter of 1982–83. Batting on a dodgy wicket in Launceston, Tasmania, he was hit an awful blow in the mouth by Michael Holding and from that day on I have felt that he has never been the same against genuinely quick bowling. With just a little more faith in himself he might well have grown out of that fear over the years but sadly he has never been quite the same batsman since that fateful day. Some critics have suggested that injury, which forced him to miss six weeks of the tour, is also a reason for his nervous disposition but there is a much simpler explanation. He is addicted to strong black coffee, often drinking more than fifteen cups a day, and it's no wonder that with all that caffeine inside him he is always on edge and that he can't sleep properly at night.

'On edge' would be a kind way of describing Randall's state of mind during the Lord's final and after running out his captain, guilt put him under even greater pressure. Another mid-wicket misunderstanding saw Evans run out and, although Randall made 49, he cracked in the penultimate over when he slogged Derek Pringle rashly into the hands of Mark Waugh on the leg-side boundary with only ten runs wanted.

So Bruce French and I began the last over with nine runs wanted with Lever, backed by two decades of experience and achievement, the bowler, Bruce and I hared between the wickets scrambling two singles, a bye to the wicketkeeper, and picking up a couple to the boundary at square-leg. The noisy Essex fans gratefully appreciated the fact that I couldn't score off the fifth ball so the final reached its climax with a boundary needed off the last.

As if the tension was not bad enough Graham Gooch was determined to try and fray my nerves as much as possible consulting with his whole team for three minutes over his field placings and then discovering just as Lever was coming in to bowl that he had not got the necessary four fielders inside the circle. More adjustments and it became clear that Lever intended to bowl a yorker on my leg stump which is the hardest of all deliveries to smack away for four, especially since Gooch had packed the leg-side boundary with fielders.

My one hope was to swing the bat from inside the line and try to squeeze the ball away on the off side. The battle with Lever was rather like two Western gunfighters sizing up to each other at high noon. He knew and I knew the obvious thing for him was a yorker. But because it was so obvious would it be a yorker? It was like a football goalkeeper guessing at a penalty. I had to make my mind up before his arm came over and I did. Before he bowled I moved my legs away to get ready for the carve. I had guessed right; it was sheer luck, because if it had not been a yorker I would have looked an absolute idiot. I wouldn't have been in the same street as the ball let alone the same cricket ground!

I made contact, though I wouldn't claim it was off the middle of the bat, and as the ball sliced away just backward of square on the off side, Bruce and I set off running and we had completed two before I dared look to see what was happening with the ball. Travelling up the hill towards the boundary below the Lord's grandstand it was taking an eternity to reach the ropes and Brian Hardie was chasing it as though his life depended on it.

Fortunately the ball just won the race and Bruce French and I wrapped our arms around each other and waltzed back to the pavilion in joy. I look for Lever afterwards and couldn't find him. I think he just slid away because he knew it was probably his last appearance at Lord's before retirement and clinching the final for Essex would have been a fitting farewell to one of the game's great characters and competitors. Obviously I felt for him; I wouldn't have liked it had the positions been reversed as they so easily could have been.

There is a hell of a lot of luck in cricket!

9

FIGHTING BACK

There can hardly have been a more controversial or depressing period for English cricket than the summer of 1989 when two major issues kept the sport prominently in big headlines on the sports pages and occasionally on the front pages as well. On the field we were being hammered to all parts by the Australians while off it there were constant rumours, which were confirmed early in August, that there was to be another rebel tour of English players to South Africa. For the most part I stayed largely on the sidelines on both issues mainly because of one man, John Emburey.

Although I had flogged my way around the World Cup, Pakistan and New Zealand with a measure of success and been chosen in the winter of 1988–89 for the England tour to India that was cancelled when the government there objected to the South African connections of some members of the party, I was still regarded as second in line behind the Middlesex off spinner when the Australian series got underway and had not actually played in the England side for nearly eighteen months. It was only after the Ashes had already been lost with defeat in the Manchester Test, which coincided with the exposure of the rebel tour – in which Emburey was a leading character – that the selectors turned to me to play in the fifth Test at Trent Bridge.

It was hardly surprising that while names were being touted all over the place mine did not feature in the rebels' plans. With Emburey part of the organisation and Gloucestershire's left-arm spinner David Graveney appointed the tour's player/manager there was certainly no room in the sixteen-strong party for a third slow bowler and I know I would not have accepted an invitation to visit the Republic even if one had been forthcoming.

A fee of around £40,000 a winter for two years was far more money than I had ever earned in the game. But since my earliest days on the Warwickshire staff it had always been my ambition to play for England and even if Test match fees, which rose dramatically after the Kerry Packer revolution, had been £15 instead of £1,500 and there was only the vaguest of chances of me playing another Test I would have done nothing to jeopardise those prospects. Three of my colleagues at Trent Bridge – Chris Broad, Tim Robinson and Bruce French – did however decide to go and they left me with mixed feelings.

Putting aside all political considerations because any pro-fessional cricketer should, like businessmen, be free to earn money wherever they can, I know that both Broad and Robinson felt that joining the rebels was a one-off oppor-tunity to secure a sound financial future for their families. They both had also suffered over the years at the hands of the selectors with no guarantees that either would play Test cricket again. But I couldn't help but feel that, a year before Mike Atherton and Graham Gooch were to establish them-selves as England's opening pair, they had turned their backs on Test cricket prematurely. Both were proven Test players with good records and over the years I had come to regard them as one of the best opening pairs in county cricket.

Bruce French on the other hand was an entirely different case. He had been desperately unlucky to lose his England place some 15 months earlier, when, barely a week before the start of the start of the 1988 home series against the West Indies, he had been forced to enter hospital for surgery. He had spent the previous winter on tour with us carrying a very sore finger which had begun to affect his performances. When X-rays revealed that the joint was so shattered it would not repair naturally, French had little option but to have an operation to fuse the bone back together. By the time he was ready to return to county cricket in late August, England had dabbled with Jack Richards and Paul Downton against the West Indies and were about to give Jack Russell a chance to make his mark in the final Test of the summer against Sri Lanka.

A season later while everyone else was losing their heads in the early matches against the Australians, Jack not only performed well with the gloves but also began to score useful runs in a losing cause, and there were a lot of other younger wicketkeepers in the queue behind him. So by the time the South African option came around there seemed no way back for French and I felt sorry for him.

I may be biased having played alongside French day in and day out since I first signed for Notts, but for me there was no better gloveman in the country at the time. Russell is a fine wicketkeeper but playing with Gloucestershire over the years he had little or no opportunity to keep wicket to an off spinner. French, however, knows my bowling inside out and although I have lost count of the number of times when on a bouncing and turning wicket he has cursed me as a ball has spun viciously through the gate to hit him painfully on the chest, arms or even head, he is a master of his art. He has certainly been well worth more than the sixteen caps he accumulated before that untimely operation.

Once details of the South African tour party were made public on the final morning of the Manchester Test, the Test and County Cricket Board, knowing there would be an outcry worldwide, had little option other than to say that all the players involved would not be considered for the final two Tests of the Ashes series and that paved the way for me to win another England cap at Trent Bridge. I had been asked to Lord's by Micky Stewart for a two-day get-together for the England squad in mid-April, but that was the nearest I had been to a place in the side for a long time.

I suppose in the unreal world of *Boy's Own* comics a recall to the England side for a 40-year-old would automatically be followed by a heroic match-winning performance. If only that had been the case. There was little romance for any of us English bowlers as the Aussie openers, Geoff Marsh and Mark Taylor, broke all kinds of records putting on 329 for their first wicket and their total when the declaration finally arrived on the Saturday was 602 for 9 declared, leaving us to bat out the next three days to save the game.

While my bowling had hardly set the world alight since I went wicketless in 33 overs, at least there was some consolation with the bat and I was second highest scorer in each of our two innings, making 38 and 35. But it was during the second knock as we were heading for a large innings defeat that I had a run-in with Geoff Lawson which made the headlines in the next morning's papers. The problem started when I edged the fast bowler in the direction of Steve Waugh in the slips who claimed the catch.

My normal policy is that if I nick the ball I walk instantly, but on this occasion there was doubt over whether the ball had carried and since the umpire immediately said 'not out' I stayed my ground. Lawson was absolutely furious as he stood in the middle of the pitch telling me and anyone else who cared to listen what he thought of the decision. With some fairly robust hitting I was starting to build a useful score when we left the field for tea. But as we approached the pavilion, Lawson started having another go at me. I have heard worse things on the pitch playing local soccer, but I shut him up simply by turning round in his direction and asking, 'Have you got a problem, son?' The whole incident was a pity really because over the years I have enjoyed playing the Aussies – they like to play the game hard and give no quarter but while they invented the art of sledging it rarely goes any further. Once the umpire has made his decision they normally get straight on with the game.

We lost the Test by an innings and 180 runs and while I was picked for the final squad of twelve to play the sixth Test at the Oval the selectors chose to go in with only one spinner, Nick Cook, thus continuing the pattern of my international career, where to that point I had never been given a settled run in the side. There was some small compensation, however, in that without saying I would definitely be in the winter tour parties for the Nehru Cup in India and the West Indies at the start of 1990, it was hinted that with Emburey out of the way England had no other off spinner in their sights.

Everyone knew that travelling to the West Indies for a three-month tour in the New Year was going to be hard. The shattering defeat at the hands of the Australians had left English cricket at rock bottom in the eyes of many critics and with the South African saga taking away several top players who might have been in the tour party we hardly looked strong on paper. Yet in the four months between the end of the English season and our departure for the Caribbean so much hard work was put in by everyone concerned we were able to spring a few surprises, not least of all winning the first Test in Jamaica.

To outperform everybody's expectations in the West Indies we needed a complete overhaul of attitudes towards our Test cricket and that meant starting at the top with the people at Lord's and filtering down throughout the system.

Micky Stewart had been the manager ever since the 1986–87 tour to Australia when we won the Ashes under Mike Gatting and I know it was a terrible loss to him when Mike had to be sacked. We had some successes at the World Cup in 1987 but I felt all along that Micky was trying to do the job with one hand tied behind his back. The TCCB had, for the first time, agreed to a full-time manager of the England team and yet, given the continued existence of a committee of selectors, he obviously could not rule with a completely free hand.

Stewart also inherited many players whose approach to the game had been formed over the previous ten years and he struggled on the basis that you cannot 'teach old dogs new tricks' to get his ideas over. Just how bad things had been in the English camp struck me quickly on my first-ever overseas tour to Australia in 1982–83. I had always regarded training and hard practice as an integral part of a professional cricketer's life since my early days at Edgbaston. Yet during that first winter in Australia I was amazed at the completely amateurish attitude towards the nets where it was a case of players almost being asked, 'Well, what would you like to do now?' The almost inevitable consequence was that those players who found nets a tiresome bore would find other ways of spending their days off, fishing, sailing or going out with groups of friends for lunchtime sessions that hindered rather than helped their fitness.

It was well illustrated on that tour in Sydney when we stayed at the luxurious Sebel Town House set on a hillside just barely 100 yards from the edge of the city's lively King's Cross district. From our bedroom windows, just down the hill was a delightful little cricket ground ideal for a spot of extra training and barely two minutes' run away from our hotel. Yet the lure of the Cross attracted several of the players and whenever I visited that ground for an extra run I was usually on my own. On the rare occasions when I saw someone actually using the nets, it was our press boys trying to get into some sort of shape for their occasional matches with their Australian counterparts.

At nights, too, Australia provided far too many distractions. While I would like to prepare for a game with a quiet meal in my room watching TV, others would be out in the bars or restaurant or enjoying barbecues in private houses. I say all this with no disrespect to Doug Insole who was our manager on that tour, his assistant Norman Gifford or Bob

Willis the skipper; after all, legend has it that Denis Compton used to turn up for games still wearing his dinner jacket from the night before! It had been the system for a long time and it was to take Stewart a couple of years before it could be overhauled.

The words 'optional nets' were to become a joke in the West Indies under David Gower in 1986, but once Ted Dexter took over from Peter May at the head of the selection process and his newly formed England committee presented a much more 'slimline' approach based mainly around Stewart and the relevant captain, changes had to come. The background to David Gower leading England in the 1989 Ashes disaster ahead of apparent first choice Mike Gatting was of no concern to me, but once Gatting had aligned himself with the South African tour it was a masterstroke to turn to Graham Gooch for the West Indies.

Gooch has always been a quiet man in the dressing room, not without a sense of humour, but never the boisterous type. He will always have a firm word in the ear of a player when it is necessary but he will never bawl one out in public. As a cricketer he is a complete professional, working harder than anyone on fitness and constantly making little adjustments to his batting in the nets in search of perfection. Although hardly an inspirational tactician in the Mike Brearley mould, he has vast personal experience to call upon when making his decisions which are sound more often than not. What was so interesting was the choice of Allan Lamb as vice-captain.

As personalities Gooch and Lamb are almost like chalk and cheese. For all the quiet calculated approach of the skipper, Lamb is a constant bundle of energy who can barely stay still for a second and I am sure he regards sleep as a waste of time in his life's-for-living philosophy. I think that, rather unfairly, too much has been made over the years of Lamb's way of life and too little attention paid to his qualities as a cricketer. To go out as he has done over the years and score six centuries against the West Indies' fast bowlers takes more than just ability, it takes raw courage. There have been many occasions when Lamb's name has been linked with events off the field, but on the field he is 100 per cent effort and never more so than when someone has criticised him. I think he is one of those really great players who, whenever everyone else in the side finds themselves up against a wall, tends to come shining through.

The combination of Stewart, Lamb and Gooch began to pay instant dividends on our trip to India for the Nehru Cup. There had not been a big enough gap since the end of the English season for the players to shrug off fully their tiredness or forget the memories of the Ashes series. But it was quickly made clear to us in the early practice sessions that we had not gone to the sub-continent just for a holiday. They made us work hard and put in a great deal of effort off the field building a new team spirit – and the results began to show. Among our early games was a welcome victory over the Aussies at Hyderabad and against all expectations we comfortably reached the semi-finals of the tournament before losing to a strong Pakistan side in Nagpur.

If the Indian excursion did more for team spirit than anything else in the two months back home prior to departure for the Caribbean, we quickly discovered that the management had thought up a tough routine to prepare us for the encounter with Malcolm Marshall and his friends.

I had ricked my back in India and a short bout of 'flu soon after we returned from England set back my own preparations but by mid-December I had trimmed down from thirteen and a half stone to twelve stone ten pounds which was the lightest I had been since the 1970s. I had never been one to go in for long-distance road running, preferring to do a little bit of work often and as the weeks went by I cut five minutes off the time for a three-mile run I used to do in a park near our home.

While I have always enjoyed a pint, a period of enforced

abstinence helped me get into trim and twice a week I drove up to Headingley for nets with some of the other northern-based England players. By the time we got together for a week at Lilleshall with the England 'A' team squad which was heading for Zimbabwe I was fitter than I had ever been. Obviously I couldn't expect to outpace the youngsters in the squads, there would have been something wrong with them if I could, but I met all the targets set down for me by the specialist fitness instructors brought in by Stewart to assist with our preparations.

As things turned out I was left with quite a bit of free time in the West Indies since the tour selectors decided to match fire with fire playing four seamers in the first Test at Jamaica. When we won that match against all the predictions they decided there was little point in changing a winning policy just for the sake of it. In addition they were well aware that the West Indies were unlikely to produce turning wickets when their greatest strength lay in their own fast bowling.

On St Lucia for our second tour game, however, Keith Medlycott and I nearly managed to bowl us to astonishing victory over the Windward Islands. A previously unknown spinner, Mervyn Durand, had caused our batsmen all sorts of problems and had forced us to follow on behind their 317 all out. Allan Lamb and David Capel fought back in our second innings but we still only left the Windwards to score 139 for victory. After an early strike by Phil DeFreitas, Gooch left it to us two spinners to try to retrieve something from the game and by applying steady pressure we took four wickets each before the Islanders achieved a well-earned victory with one wicket to spare.

Although I played in all our one-day games on the tour and also in the Island game against Jamaica, most of my time was spent retaining a level of fitness should my services be required. Although we had a tremendous team spirit there were times when my age set me apart from the rest since I had been playing first-class cricket at the time when young-sters like Devon Malcolm and Angus Fraser were still in nappies! It was Fraser who started calling me 'Fossil' and in the evenings when the youngsters went out in search of their own entertainment, although nothing was ever said, I felt they'd be happier without an old man like me around. I found myself, as had been the case in India, usually dining with a member of the management team, either with Ste-wart, manager Peter Lush or our physio Laurie Brown. And to be honest, because they were more my age group, I pre-ferred their level of conversation. But the fact that I was eating most nights with two of the selectors had no bearing on whether I would play in the Tests or not.

At the end of the tour when hopes of victory in the series, which had risen so high after winning in Jamaica and were almost fulfilled in Trinidad where we were robbed by the rain, had been flattened, Lamb had to take tremendous stick over his captaincy in the final two Tests at Barbados and Antigua which we lost.

It was said that had Gooch not so tragically had his finger broken by Ezra Moseley on that electric final day in Trinidad we would not have been beaten. The critics shared the blame between the poor form of some of our batsmen and Lamb's leadership. It was a harsh judgement against Lamb.

Although any tour vice-captain is, to a certain extent, appointed in the expectation that he would be capable of taking over the leadership if called upon in an emergency, I think Lambie was mainly and rightly chosen to be the ideal foil to Gooch, in the hope that his endless enthusiasm would rub off on some of the younger players. The selectors knew that as a captain he had only been leading Northants for one season and that his experiences at home in the summer of 1989 had been strictly limited by a series of injuries.

If I had one criticism of Lamb in that last couple of weeks of a dramatic tour, it must also be levelled at the other selectors and that was the fact that I did not play in those last two Tests. I know people say that Gooch's broken finger cost us the series, but I think just as damaging to us was the rib-muscle injury that ruled Angus Fraser out of those last two games.

Although only a youngster Fraser had shown with his five-wicket haul in the first innings at Kingston that his height and movement and most importantly his accuracy were vital ingredients of our attack against free-stroke playing batsmen on the fast bouncy wickets in the Caribbean. With Fraser on the sidelines Lamb had no one to call upon to put the cork back in the bottle once the West Indian batsmen got on top in those final two Tests. There was no way of telling how I might have done given that neither Barbados nor Antigua is traditionally a happy hunting ground for spinners. But I do feel my experience ahead of four young quick bowlers in their twenties might have helped Lamb through the more difficult periods. If I was considered good enough to contain the West Indies in the more frantic atmosphere of one-day games, then it must have been worth a try in those two Tests. But as we flew home to face the challenge of a new summer I was as uncertain as ever about my Test future. The rapid progress made by the team as a whole, however, meant that the previous year's Ashes disasters had been more or less forgotten and the long-awaited new dawn for English cricket, achieved through hard work and professionalism, was about to break.

10

THE COMING OF AGE

Spending three months at the beginning of 1990 with England in the West Indies was a very mixed experience. After thinking for so long that English Test cricket was never going to progress far while it revolved around an amateur set-up, the tough training regime introduced by Micky Stewart and Graham Gooch in the weeks leading up to that tour was more than welcome, yet to spend all five Tests as twelfth man and play only in the one-day internationals was a frustrating experience.

Still, I returned to England for the summer knowing that with three Tests to be played against both New Zealand and India it was almost certain that, barring a disastrous loss of form, I would get two or three more caps. Keith Medlycott, the young Surrey left-arm spinner who had been sent to the Caribbean, was not going to be a major threat immediately. Micky Stewart had asked me to try to help Keith on the tour and we worked hard together in the nets. Although he was naturally a big spinner of the ball I tried to get him to bowl the ball a bit faster since when the ball wasn't turning a great deal he looked ripe for a batsman willing to have a go. In terms of experience Medlycott improved during the tour but he was still some way short of making the Test side and since there was no young off spinner anywhere near the horizon challenging me for a place, I was confident that England would need me during the summer.

However given that seven years has elapsed since my

debut and the fact that I had played only nine previous Tests and never more than two in succession, I could not in my wildest expectations foresee myself being picked to play in all six games.

I had lost count of the number of times I had been named in an England twelve only to be the odd man left out when the balance of the attack was decided just before the start of a Test. Those couple of hours in the early morning leading up to the start are very nerve-wracking for any player who is only on the fringes of the team and not guaranteed selection. We all know that the basic line-up is usually decided by the selectors on the eve of the game, but they tend to keep their options open until the last minute in case they change their minds about the state of the wicket after it has had a final mow and roll on the morning of the game.

Occasionally the captain will quietly single out the luckless individual first thing in the dressing room while we are changing before practice. More often than not it happens on the outfield with an arm slid around the shoulder and an attempt at comfort with the words, 'I am sorry old boy, but maybe next time.' Some more nervous individuals have gone to great lengths to avoid catching the captain's eye during the exercises, but there is no escape.

Before the Tests we had the normal one-day internationals against the Kiwis and even though spinners rarely feature in England plans at Headingley I got the nod. The match was a great disappointment for English fans who had expected so much seeing us back in action for the first time after the West Indies trip. With Robin Smith scoring a tremendous 128 our total of 295 should have been way out of the Kiwis' reach but we all, myself included, bowled badly and Mark Greatbatch's unbeaten 102 saw them home with a ball to spare. My mind flickered back briefly to the World Series Cup game at Adelaide on my first tour to Australia when New Zealand had also managed to overhaul an enormous total; still, we quickly overcame the disappointment to square the series at the Oval despite another Greatbatch century and so moved on to the first Test at Trent Bridge.

Had Chris Lewis not reported with a migraine which prevented him making his debut, I might not have made the game though I desperately wanted to play in front of my own crowd again. In the event the weather made the whole match totally inconclusive. I was given 19 overs in the Kiwis' first innings and at least ended Greatbatch's fine little trot when he played around a straight ball and was bowled for just a single, but it was hardly the sort of performance that made my place a certainty when we moved on to Lord's for the second encounter a fortnight later.

The game was preceded by the announcement that Richard Hadlee was to be knighted for his services to cricket. Given that he had virtually carried the New Zealand attack on his shoulders for more than a decade and after a slightly petulant youth had been seen as a clean-cut ambassador for the game, it was thoroughly deserved. Although I was delighted for him I would not say we had been the best of friends in the dressing room during his time at Trent Bridge. While I admired him tremendously as a cricketer and respected all that he did for the county and New Zealand I found him a very cold character. He had his own exceedingly high standards and was not all that tolerant of other players with lesser ability. As a senior player with so much knowledge he should have helped the younger players more. He was to say later that no one at Notts ever approached him for help, yet I remember the one occasion when Andy Pick did ask for his help. Richard simply replied, 'Ninety per cent of cricket is in the head' and walked away. Yet Andy, a cricketer of genuine but limited ability, should have benefited more from being in the same dressing room as such a fine player. I think Richard only really felt happy when he was talking cricket with his equals.

Still, Richard worked very hard on his public image over the years and his great honour received widespread approval

111

– no one could ever take away from his world record of 431 Test wickets most of which he captured after fighting his way back after serious injuries and also ignoring his advancing years. And now that he was going into his last game on the hallowed turf at Lord's boosted by such an honour it didn't take a genius to work out that he would be firing on all cylinders.

For all concerned however, the game turned out to be an even greater damp squib than the first encounter at Trent Bridge, although Richard and I had an interesting tussle. He bowled me for a duck in our first innings of 334 and then when he had made 86 I earned my revenge as the Kiwis replied with 462 for 9 declared. Hadlee had been in magnificent form crashing two sixes and 12 fours on his way to what looked a certain farewell century but he tried to swing across the line once too often and I bowled him. He left the field to an emotional round of applause from the huge Lord's crowd and turned around saluting each part of the ground in turn. I doubt whether there was an English supporter sitting in the ground who would have begrudged him a century and I do not suppose I was too popular for taking his wicket but as far as I was concerned it was a Test match and there was no room for sentiment on my part.

In the days leading up to the announcement of the twelve for the final Test of the series at Edgbaston there was considerable debate in the press about my future in the side. Reporters were claiming that I hadn't bowled well at Lord's although taking 2 for 67 in 30 overs was not exactly an expensive return. What many of the critics were quick to point out was the fact that I had only taken nineteen wickets in my previous eleven Tests and had yet actually to bowl a side out.

What many of them did not realise was that on almost all of the previous occasions that I had been bowling for England I had been acting under the strictest of captain's instruction and used generally in a defensive role. As anyone at Notts could have told those critics, I like to be considered as an attacking bowler and when given my head enjoy nothing more than giving the ball a bit of air to tease the batsmen. But bowling for England I would not dream of disobeying a skipper – for a start I could not afford to. I had never established myself as a permanent member of the team and had gone into all my previous games playing for my place. But all the time the press were calling for my head I have to say that never once did an England captain come up to me and complain about my performances.

I am not one of those cricketers who constantly moan at the members of the press. For a start they have a difficult job to do and secondly I rarely read newspapers and when I do I never look at the cricket pages. During an English summer anyway with the constant cycle of Test matches, tourists' matches and one-day competitions between the Tests, the leading writers, who follow England around the globe for twelve months of the year, get very few opportunities actually to go back to the grass roots and watch a Championship game. Had many of the critics been able to watch Nottinghamshire more over the years they would have seen that at county level, unless specifically directed otherwise, I always bowl in an attacking mode.

Going back to Birmingham to face the Kiwis obviously meant a lot to me. Making the final eleven also created a bit of personal history for it would be the first occasion when I would be playing three matches on the trot for England and there were still many local people at the Warwickshire club who I was convinced had never seen the best of Eddie Hemmings. Once again, however, the rain did its best to intervene – it was a perverse fact, in a summer which will long be remembered as one of the hottest for years and breaking so many records, that whatever rain fell during June and July it tended to be during the Test matches.

Play did not begin until after lunch on the first day and when Kiwi skipper John Wright won the toss he asked us to bat hoping that moisture in the air and in the wicket would assist Hadlee in what was to be his final Test match. It proved to be an error of judgement as Graham Gooch, who was back to his best after the heartbreak of his broken finger in the West Indies, and Mike Atherton, overcoming his first-innings duck at Lord's, put on 170 for the first wicket in only three and a half hours. They had more than made up for the lost time, but a middle order collapse on the second day threatened to rob us of a commanding total. It was left to us tail-end Charlies to rescue England and useful contributions from Jack Russell, Chris Lewis and Gladstone Small, not forgetting my own 20, meant that the last four wickets added 119 runs and our final score of 435 put us in the driving seat.

Although Devon Malcolm got one ball on the Friday night to rear nastily and strike Trevor Franklyn a painful blow on the head, there didn't seem to be a great deal of danger in the wicket as the Kiwis began their reply. Nevertheless Malcolm had both John Wright and Andrew Jones caught behind in the Saturday morning session which saw us attacking throughout with the seamers and I didn't expect to get too many overs before their second innings.

My break came, however, when Gladstone Small, who was struggling to get anything out of the pitch, complained that the ball was getting soft and suggested that I might give the opposition a bit more trouble. The next few hours were to present me with my first real taste of success as a Test bowler.

For once I was allowed to bowl with a big first-innings total at my back and also there was no captain telling me to keep it tight at all costs. Graham Gooch gave me my head backed up by attacking fields and there is nothing that encourages me more than the sight of close fields clustering around the bat. Although the pitch was only offering me slow turn, there was a little bounce in the pitch and suddenly I was on a hot run.

Franklyn, ignoring the headache that was a legacy from the night before, jabbed forward and Robin Smith gobbled up a catch at silly point. Hadlee spent half an hour scoring eight before edging one to slip where Mike Atherton took a fine diving catch. John Bracewell tried to answer back with a belligerent knock that yielded 25 off only 22 balls, but then backed away to hit me through the covers, missed and was bowled. When Ken Rutherford edged a bat-pad catch to Alec Stewart at short-leg I had taken four wickets for the first time in a Test and was beginning to show the knockers how I could bowl when the circumstances were in my favour.

At 230–8 the Kiwis still needed 13 to avoid the follow-on and I was unable to stop Martin Snedden and Mark Parore seeing them past the danger mark but before the close I had Snedden lbw and bowled Danny Morrison to wrap up their innings for 249 and finish with figures of 6–58 from 27.3 overs.

As we left the field I got a standing ovation from the Warwickshire members and I couldn't have been more delighted to have produced my most profitable Test return in front of them. With the Sunday rest day to follow I was able to go out and celebrate in the evening happier in the knowledge that my Test career which had been under threat was in line for an extension. A study of the scorecard from that innings also gave me professional pride for the way the wickets had been taken.

Apart from Bracewell's wild swing all the rest of my victims had either been bowled, fallen lbw or been taken by catches close to the wicket which was a sign that my bowling had been tight, keeping the batsmen consistently under pressure and gradually winkling them out.

Although I was still not taking England selection for granted I would have been surprised to have been left out as the international programme against India got under way with one-day internationals at Leeds and Nottingham. Those

England 435 (G A Gooch 154, M A Atherton 82)

New Zealand first innings:

T J Franklyn c Smith b Hemmings	....	66
J G Wright c Russell b Malcolm	....	24
A H Jones c Russell b Malcolm	....	2
M D Crowe lbw b Lewis	....	11
M J Greatbatch lbw b Malcolm	....	45
K R Rutherford c Stewart b Hemmings	....	29
Sir Richard Hadlee c Atherton b Hemmings	....	8
J G Bracewell b Hemmings	....	25
A C Parore not out	....	12
M C Snedden lbw b Hemmings	....	2
D K Morrison b Hemmings	....	1
Extras (b9, lb11, w2, nb2)	....	24
Total	....	249

Fall: 1/45 2/67 3/90 4/161 5/163 6/185 7/223 8/230 9/243
Bowling: Small 18–7–44–0 Malcolm 25–7–59–3 Lewis 19–5–55–1
Hemmings 27.3–10–58–6 Atherton 9–5–17–0

two games quickly brought home to us that our second opponents were going to present far stiffer opposition than the Kiwis. At Headingley we asked them to score 230 and they knocked off the runs with only four wickets down and while Robin Smith scored a great century as we made 281 at Trent Bridge the Indians knocked them off with two overs to spare. With experienced batsmen like Mohammad Azharuddin, Ravi Shastri and Dilip Vengsarkar backed up by the precocious talent of seventeen-year-old Sachin Tendulkar, who was being hailed as the heir-apparent to Sunil Gavaskar, they possessed a tremendous depth to their batting.

But then we, too, were growing in confidence and with Graham Gooch enjoying a magnificent summer with the bat, the stage was set for an interesting confrontation as the first Test began at Lord's. No one could have foreseen that one of the most dramatic Tests in the history of the game was about to be played.

After Azharuddin had gambled by asking us to bat first, few captains have played a more inspirational innings for

116

their side than the 333 scored by Gooch. Although he was dropped on 36 when the Indian wicketkeeper Kiran More spilled a straightforward catch off Sanjeev Sharma, the crowd were richly entertained for ten hours. It was only immense tiredness that saw him drive outside the line of a full-length delivery from Manoj Prabhakar when he was within 32 runs of the world record Test score of 365 set by Sir Gary Sobers in the winter of 1957–58. With Allan Lamb and Robin Smith both scoring centuries we reached 653 for 4 declared and for the second match running I knew that at some stage I would have the luxury of bowling with a big total in the bank, though on a perfect Lord's wicket with India's talented line-up it was going to be no easy task.

For the major part of India's reply Gooch relied on our three seamers Malcolm, Lewis and Gus Fraser who gradually worked their way through the innings, though I did make one valuable contribution with the wicket of Ravi Shastri who, after thwarting us with a fine century, charged down the wicket and slammed me straight into the hands of the skipper at mid-on.

Azharuddin tried to make amends to his team-mates for the blunder of asking us to bat first by scoring a fluent century and when the game entered its fourth morning it was by no means certain that we were going to be able to enforce the follow-on which looked our best route to victory. Fortunately the Indian captain only added four more to his overnight 117 when I found a way past his defence and when Fraser claimed the wickets of More and Sharma in quick succession only one more recognised batsman stood in our way.

Kapil Dev had made it clear from the moment he walked to the crease that he intended to try to blast the Indians to safety and he had already made 48 in double quick time when their last man Narendra Hirwani joined him out in the middle with 24 runs still required to make England bat again immediately. With all due respect to the young leg

117

spinner, Hirwani's lack of ability with the bat would force him to struggle to get in higher than eleven in many club sides and Kapil was well aware that it might only take one ball to end the innings.

As I came in to bowl to Kapil from the Nursery End he sized up the first two balls with defensive strokes before launching me over the ropes for six with a fierce drive. I wasn't discouraged because I knew that he was taking risks and that if I kept the ball in the right spot it would only take a slight error of judgement on the batsman's behalf to give me his wicket. Kapil and I had crossed swords in similar fashion at Bombay in the World Cup and the large Indian contingent in the crowd rose off their seats with a deafening roar as Kapil drove the next ball even higher and harder up onto the scaffolding of the new Nursery End stand that was nearing completion behind my back.

Yet another record was added to the many that had already been broken in the game as Kapil launched the next two balls for six in the same direction – the first time any batsman had achieved four successive sixes in a Test – and his powerful display of hitting had saved the follow-on. His thinking was totally justified since from the first ball of the next over Fraser trapped the hapless Hirwani lbw to wrap up the Indian innings.

It was only after the third six had been struck that Gooch wandered over to me and had a quiet word, but there was little he could say. All four deliveries had been bowled exactly as I had planned and would have been met by a more cautious batsman under any other circumstances with a defensive prod. But Kapil had set his mind on trying to avoid the follow-on in that over and as long as he played the shots perfectly there was nothing I could do about it – the rules did not allow bowlers to have a fielder situated ten rows back in the stands! But Kapil had played with only the smallest margin of error as I was able to prove 24 hours later.

Despite the barrage we still had a first-innings lead of 199 and with Gooch scoring another brilliant century to take his match aggregate to a record 456 were able to set the Indians a target of 472 to win in seven hours. That too would have required an effort of record-breaking proportions, but since the Lord's wicket was still playing like a dream there was no logical reason why the Indians should not have batted out the remainder of the match to secure a draw. In the event they decided to play their natural game and it proved their downfall. Furthermore I was bowling again when Kapil came to the crease. For the second time in the match he decided to take me on only this time, faced with a delivery that was bowled no differently from any of those four in the first innings, when he went for another six he mis-hit the ball slightly and gave a catch to Chris Lewis at deep mid-wicket. The ball had turned just enough to miss the middle of the bat. If that had happened to any one of the four a day earlier we might never have needed a second innings and I would have been spared some pretty savage criticism in the papers.

There was more to follow in the second Test at Old Trafford when yet another Gooch century and our second-innings declaration left the Indians to score 405 to win in a full day and 25 minutes. At one stage on the final day we looked to be cruising to victory as they slumped to 127 for 5 and we were still in the driving-seat nearly 50 runs later when Kapil, after hitting a quick-fire 26, decided yet again to have a big lunge at me, missed and was bowled. But from then on we were thwarted in an unbroken stand of 160 between the teenager Tendulkar, who showed a maturity way beyond his age on his way to a maiden century, and Prabhakar. Much of the blame for us failing to force home a winning position was heaped on my head, for when Tendulkar had made only ten he danced down the wicket and smashed a return catch to my right which I failed to hold on to and thereafter he did not offer another chance. But with the power he had put into the shot I thought I had shown pretty sharp reactions even to get a hand to the ball.

From their fighting draw at Old Trafford the Indians recovered to force us onto the back foot in the final match of the series at the Oval when batting first they scored 606 for 9 declared. There had been some speculation as to whether I would keep my place in the side not so much because of the incidents at Lord's and Old Trafford but more because England might have been tempted to play four seamers on the hard Oval wicket. The selectors, however, stood by me and while all of us bowlers took a fair amount of stick I gained another ounce of revenge by having Kapil smartly stumped by Jack Russell. That strike and the wicket of Anil Wason gave me eleven victims in the series – which was won since two more great innings by Gooch secured us a draw – and I was second leading wicket-taker behind Fraser and second in the averages. In fact I had taken 21 wickets in the summer, more than double my tally for the previous seven years, and at an average of just over 32 it was not a bad return in a boiling summer when bowlers all around the country were struggling to get wickets.

Since the selectors had not even given another spinner the opportunity to oust me from the side in either of the two series I felt fairly certain that I would still be in their minds for the Ashes tour to Australia, but by the end of the season I felt completely washed out. Although it should never be the case, I was almost only going through the basic motions with Notts when I reported back to the county at the end of the Oval Test to play out the last few games of the season.

I had never had the chance to realise before just how much the strain of Test cricket could take out of me. It might be argued that at the age of 41, playing two series back to back was certain to take its toll. But I had no problems with my general level of fitness and never felt it while the games were being played since the adrenalin was buzzing all the time. But playing all through the international programme was a new experience for me; had it been a regular occurrence for ten years I would still have been tired but I would have coped with it a lot better.

As it was, as soon as the season ended I put my feet up for a fortnight and did nothing whatsoever until I felt I was mentally refreshed. Then I began to do light training every day and by the time we left for the tour to Australia in mid October I was looking forward to another Ashes battle.

11

DISASTER DOWN UNDER
(Australia Tour 1990–91)

After spending the best part of 25 years attempting to reach the top in my profession, I had hoped, rather than expected, to stay there at least for a year or two. Playing in all those six Tests against New Zealand and India had, I thought, established me as the country's first-choice spinner when we left for Australia half-way through October with the target of regaining the Ashes. Once again the selectors, mainly through a continuing lack of choice among the more mature slow bowlers on the county scene, had decided that my off spin should be partnered by a young slow left armer, and as Keith Medlycott had suffered a loss of form on his return to Surrey from the Caribbean the place went to another London youngster, Phil Tufnell of Middlesex.

Tufnell had many good things going in his favour since he was playing for a county with a good spinning tradition, was working under a vastly experienced captain in Mike Gatting, and from the earliest days of his career had been able to study under Phil Edmonds and later play alongside John Emburey. While he had earned his tour ticket by taking 74 wickets in the summer – 13 more than Emburey – I did not initially regard him as a threat to my place. In the four and a half months that followed, however, Tufnell gradually overtook me in the eyes of the selectors and by the time we returned home late in February, comprehensively outplayed

122

in the Ashes and one-day competitions, one thing seemed certain – it was unlikely I would be picked for England again.

It was hard during the tour to put an exact finger on where it went wrong for me or why Tufnell gained his promotion. It was only afterwards once all the cricket had been played that I went to Graham Gooch for a chat and discovered his thinking. I outlined all my thoughts and basically he agreed with them, but there was a crunch when Gooch said that if it came down to a straight choice between myself and a younger player then he would always go for the youngster – clearly once he had decided that, and it must have been fairly early on the tour, there was nothing I could have done about it.

It was galling to return to England and learn from friends that I had been made one of the scapegoats for our failures. Most of the media critics were saying that neither myself nor Wayne Larkins should have been taken on the trip in the first place. Strangely enough I agreed with that sentiment when the tour party was first picked the previous September. It did seem ludicrous that at the age of 41 I should be England's first-choice spinner, but it wasn't my fault that I had been picked throughout the previous summer and had responded with a fair degree of success.

If anyone was to blame it was the county administrators and captains for their treatment of young spinners over the previous decade. They had not produced the steady supply of young slow bowlers to challenge me for my place. The critics should have launched into the system and not the individuals when the squad was announced, but after successes in the New Zealand and India Test series no one seemed to raise an eyebrow.

It was only once the Ashes had been lost that they turned sour on Wayne and myself. Yet I had only played in one of the five Tests and Wayne, whose opportunities were limited by his own injuries, had actually played well in the Melbourne Test, scoring a half century in each innings. And I don't think the critics would have said anything either if I had played throughout the series in Australia and taken say 30 wickets at an average of 25 runs apiece, but after the tour they made a lot of my age.

Unfortunately I never had a chance of returning those figures. From the moment we arrived Down Under my role in the party seemed to be more as a net bowler than a potential match winner and with Micky Stewart and Gooch continuing their policy of work, hard work and even more hard work I was to bowl hundreds, probably thousands of overs in the nets, but only be given limited opportunities to make my mark out in the middle where it really counts.

I missed our opening game against the Presidents XI at Lilac Hill, up country from Perth in Western Australia, and although picked for the two-day game against a Western Australia County XI at Geraldton I only bowled 14 overs. I played in two other one-day games in Perth and Port Pirie but missing out on the opening first-class fixture against Western Australia, it meant that the tour was almost a month old before I got my first serious bowl. That was in the State game against South Australia at the Adelaide Oval where, on one of the flattest wickets in the world, the odds are all heavily stacked in the batsman's favour. I took a wicket in the South Australia second innings, but bowling only 33 overs in the match was not enough to recapture the rhythm or confidence of the previous summer.

At that stage of the tour, however, Tufnell had not had too many opportunities either, but when he was picked ahead of me to play against an Australian X1 at Hobart in our last match before the opening Test in Brisbane, I was almost sure the writing was on the wall. Apart from my own problems things weren't going well for the team in general, and the decline had set in from the early days in Perth when Gooch suffered a hand injury which was to turn septic and keep him out of action until Christmas. It was a shattering blow to us all and more than ironic since earlier in the year it was his hand injury in Trinidad that marked the decline of our fortunes in the West Indies.

In the time it took Gooch to return to the side we also lost David Gower for a while, all-rounder Chris Lewis, who played in the Brisbane Test but then was forced to return home with a back injury, and the make-up of the squad altered with Hugh Morris flying in as temporary batting cover and later Phil DeFreitas as a permanent replacement for Lewis. All the disruptions and a series of defeats in our warm-up games against sides we should have beaten obviously took its toll on the squad as we approached that opening Test. Alarmingly for the selectors as they tried to make up for Gooch's absence, both Mike Atherton and Robin Smith, two of the younger batsmen who before the tour had begun to make such an impact on the team, had been unable to find their touch on the faster bouncier Australian wickets.

In a way, as we approached the first Test at the Gabba, I still harboured hopes of making the opening Test side. After all I had been an integral part of our summer's success, and one of the notable features of the 1990 home season was the way in which the selectors had laid much store in the continuity of team selection. If the policy had not been abandoned I should be in the frame. But missing the final warm-up game in Tasmania was an obvious warning, and it seemed from the outside that tour selectors had preconceived ideas about the teams they would play in each game. With Brisbane having a reputation for helping seamers, there was to be no place for a spinner even if that meant disturbing a winning combination. I found the change of policy very hard to handle.

I was disappointed and it wasn't easy watching from the sidelines as we went one-down in the series with the game lasting for only three of the scheduled five days. Our batting looked brittle and we were put in and then shot out in just

78 overs for 194 by Bruce Reid, who made a remarkable return to Test cricket after having a metal plate inserted in his back to strengthen his spine.

Our hearts lifted on the second day as the four-man seam attack responded by getting Australia out for 152, with Gus Fraser, Gladstone Small and Chris Lewis taking three wickets each. But much as though the bowlers strived they could not hope to win the game without runs behind them, and our second-innings collapsed to 114 all out with Terry Alderman taking six wickets setting a pattern that was to be repeated far too often on the tour.

It was a strange itinerary that then left us with virtually a month of one-day internationals in the triangular World Series Cup before our next first-class game and the second Test starting in Melbourne. We badly needed a couple of state games to get back on course and let some players return to form, but we had known the schedule well in advance and much as though we didn't like the idea, much as though we grumbled, we just had to get on with the matches that lay ahead.

Our whistle-stop tour of the states of Australia made its first touch-down at Adelaide where we opened our campaign against New Zealand. Having been a part of our one-day campaigns so often in the past I was not surprised to be in the side, but if there was to be a turning point in my tour it came soon after the match started.

I was stationed at mid on when Kiwi opener Andrew Jones pushed the ball in the midwicket area and made it clear he wanted to run two. As I picked up the ball and turned to throw I landed badly and suffered a calf muscle injury. Although I went off the field to get it strapped up by our physio Laurie Brown and returned to bowl eight overs despite the pain, it was clear I was going to miss a couple of games while the calf healed up.

From Adelaide we flew back to Perth and, given the chance to play his first one-day game for England, Tufnell grabbed it with both hands. Although he might have felt pre-match nerves he didn't show them as we took on New Zealand again, and he showed good control under pressure conceding 31 runs in his ten overs. It was not a match-winning performance but I think it caught a few eyes and after that he seemed to be the flavour of the month with the selectors.

I recovered in time to play against New Zealand at Sydney where bowling in harness with Tufnell we tied down their middle order and successfully defended our own meagre score of 194. I was dropped again as we faced the Kiwis at Brisbane, recalled to play against Australia the next day and began to realise that my high hopes for the tour were unlikely to be fulfilled.

In the week leading up to Christmas with our chances of reaching the WSC finals diminishing, we finally got back to playing four-day cricket with the game against Victoria at Ballarat. Again Tufnell was picked for the match ahead of me, though my chances of playing in the Melbourne Test on Boxing Day didn't seem too bad when Gooch had a quiet word with me and said he was quite happy with the way I was bowling.

As it turned out my hopes had been falsely raised for while I was named in the squad for the Test Tufnell got the spinner's job ahead of me. It was a decision I found hard to accept for several reasons. From the team's point of view I felt that after the Brisbane Test defeat we should go into the second game with the Aussies with as many experienced players as possible – not necessarily looking to win but determined not to lose at any costs to give us a chance to catch our breath and possibly knock the Australians out of their confident stride. Given that England was going into the game under so much pressure I didn't think it was wise to make a youngster play his first Test in such an atmosphere. I thought it would be far better for him to come in for his first cap in the third game at Sydney where the wicket would insist we play two seamers and where he could bowl in tandem with me. Then, if he was going to be an instant hit, take over the frontline role for the rest of the series.

From a personal point of view I thought I had more to offer the team. Apart from experience, I was also capable of adding runs further down the order whereas Tufnell was always going to be a tailender. I had scored runs in Australia before and in my last Test innings against India at the Oval the previous August I had scored 51. Then there was the fielding. OK at the age of 41 obviously I could not be considered as mobile as some of the younger members of the side, but there could be no doubting how hard I worked on my fitness. Tufnell on the other hand had struggled in the field and was finding himself the constant butt of barbed vocal attacks from the Aussie crowds after one or two howlers that had been replayed time and again on local TV.

It hurt me that the selectors couldn't see my point of view, and my contribution to the Melbourne Test consisted of organising the pre-play practice sessions, since Micky Stewart was forced to spend several days away from the ground suffering from a mystery virus. His health could not have been helped as we slumped to an eight-wicket defeat, our batting again letting us down in the second innings when we collapsed from 103 for one to 150 all out after earlier gaining a useful first innings lead of 46.

Despite all that had gone before it was always likely that I would play at Sydney, though my preparation for the game was not ideal. For a bowler who relies so much on rhythm I had only bowled 33 first-class overs on the tour before the start of the match. I had spent endless hours in the nets but it is not the same as middle practice – sometimes the batsmen just go out to slog you and there are never the close fielders in position to apply the pressure on which spinners often rely.

Batting first, the Australians made 518 which looked in cold light like another disaster for us. But there were mitigating factors, not least of which was the pitch, which played beautifully from the start. There there was the little matter of an incident on the Saturday when we were trying to clear up the Australian tail. Terry Alderman came forward defensively at me and pushed a catch to Alec Stewart at short leg only for umpire Peter McConnell to turn down my appeal.

Our frustration showed and I admit I was wrong to kick the ball in anger towards the stumps at the bowler's end, but the press built up the incident. I was not too happy either with the way the disciplinary issue was handled.

I was told to see manager Peter Lush at the end of the day's play and was fined £100 for my outburst. I couldn't really complain at that but the public announcements concerned me. The press were initially told that I had been dealt with and that could have been the end of the matter. But after the next day's play Micky Stewart let it be known that a second, unidentified player, had also been disciplined. I knew that had been the case but felt aggrieved that while my reprimand had been made public the identity of the second player was never disclosed.

On the field, however, I hadn't done too badly bowling Allan Border behind his legs and also picking up the wickets of Ian Healy and Carl Rackemann, finishing with three for 105 from 33 overs. I cannot say with my hand on my heart that I had bowled at my best, but I had certainly bowled worse. I did not feel quite right with my rhythm after so many weeks of inactivity and I also had a confidence problem.

That is one thing that has always been an important part of my game. At the start of the tour, with six successive Test matches under my belt, I was full of confidence, but the way things had gone in Australia had eroded everything, and I was virtually back to the apprehensive state that had marked many of my Test matches prior to the summer of 1990.

Faced with such an enormous Australian total everyone

was predicting another huge victory for the home side, with the Ashes series being wrapped up into the bargain. But after Gooch had made 59 to give our innings a solid start and after a temporary set-back with the loss of Larkins and Smith, we fought back magnificently in a partnership of 139 between Atherton and Gower.

They each scored centuries, but that was where the comparison ended. Atherton, who had slowly begun to find his feet on tour, battled bravely to reach three figures in 424 minutes, making it the slowest ton in any Test between England and Australia and also the slowest recorded in a first-class game at Sydney. Gower, despite continued pain from his hand, played one of the best innings of his Test career. He was almost brutal on the fourth morning as he exploded three fours in Alderman's first over and dealt with Rackemann just as severely. With Alec Stewart playing well for 91 and fully deserving a maiden century, after all the flak he had to take because he was the manager's son, we were able to get within 49 runs of the Aussie total before Gooch declared.

Australia faced 13 overs before the end of the day, and with Devon Malcolm producing a snorter to see off Geoff Marsh, and Mark Taylor falling lbw padding up to me, all sorts of possibilities opened up on the final morning. The wicket had begun to turn and although the ball was not going square Tufnell and I applied enough pressure to put the Aussies on the rack. After an anxious hour David Boon edged Tufnell to Gooch at slip and when the youngster struck again with successive balls to send back Border and Jones we were right on top. And it would have been even better had Gower at silly point been able to hold onto a sharp chance that would have given Tufnell a hat-trick and reduced the Australians to 129 for six only 178 ahead with more than four hours remaining.

I played my part by having Steve Waugh caught at the wicket and bowling Greg Matthews, but somehow neither of us could shift Ian Healy and Rackemann, the latter setting a new Australian record of 72 minutes getting off the mark. Happy enough to keep pushing down the wicket at either of us two slow bowlers, the big blond Queensland paceman might have been shifted earlier had Gooch resorted to pace, but he was waiting for Malcolm to feel the benefits of a pain-killing injection in his back and by the time he was introduced into the attack the match had slipped from our grasp. Although Gooch made a valiant attempt at a victory target of 255 in 28 overs it was always a Herculean task and we had to settle for a draw. With a two nil lead in the series and only two Tests to play, the Australians had retained the Ashes.

Before the fourth Test at Adelaide we still had to meet Australia in the World Series Cup to have a chance of reaching the finals, but we failed. Suddenly we had the possibility of a free week on our hands.

There were two sides to the argument as to what should have been done. The management, who of course had the final say, wanted and went ahead with organising a four-day game against New South Wales. The players wanted a rest. For those of us who had been in the West Indies the previous winter, it had been virtually unbroken cricket for 13 months, and the tiredness showed. The side as a whole was being pilloried, particularly for some of the fielding in the one-day games, but I blamed that on the tiredness. We were stale and playing stale cricket – a couple of days' break could have worked wonders.

Instead we were sent into the heart of Ned Kelly country. I have nothing personal against the town of Albury, which lies at the banks of the Murray River just inside the New South Wales border with Victoria. It is a very pleasant place with friendly people who were very keen and pleased to see us. But being so far from the coast the city tends to get hot in high summer and by hot I mean temperatures that were around 110 degrees at midday. So rather than take a much-needed break, all of us, apart from Gooch and Gower who were allowed to rest back in Melbourne, were sentenced to a game which meant absolutely nothing in conditions of extreme discomfort.

Although New South Wales beat us by six wickets, I took eight wickets in the match, including four at the start of their second innings, which just gave us an outside glimpse of victory on the final day when they required less than 100 to win.

As I had taken six wickets in the Sydney Test, I had come through two successive first-class games with fourteen victims to my name which was far better than anyone else had done at any other stage of the tour, and I was beginning to get my rhythm and confidence back. But just as I was thinking I might make the side for the fourth Test with that form behind me, I was brought down to earth with a bump.

Despite our tiredness, we left Albury at 7a.m. the day after the match to travel up to the Gold Coast for yet more practice before our final state game against Queensland. The game was made famous by the appearance of Gower and John Morris making a low pass over the ground in a light aircraft. Being left out of the side it finally occurred to me that I had no future on the England Test scene. If 14 wickets in two games was not going to be considered sufficient form to play in the Adelaide Test, then I could never hope to get back into the side.

I have no bitterness towards Tufnell, good luck to him, though his eccentric character may well get him into a few hairy positions in the future.

If I had any regrets as I went through the last few weeks of the tour, playing in only one limited-overs game on a short tour to New Zealand that was tagged onto the end of the Ashes series, it was being picked to go to Australia in the first place.

As I said earlier when the squad was first announced, English cricket should not have got itself into a position where a 41-year-old was the first-choice spinner. But given that the situation existed and I was handed my air ticket I would have expected to have played more cricket, otherwise another youngster should have been sent who could have learned a lot watching from the sidelines. I went to Australia to play a lot of cricket and, since I spent more time doing 12th man duties, on the whole it was a miserable experience. Losing the Ashes series was a great blow to us all, but personally having striven for so long to establish myself in the Test team the speed of my departure was shattering.

The tour had been a disaster from the moment Graham Gooch was injured and from then on we were never able to pick from a full-strength squad. It was interesting to see that as the fifth Test was drawing to a close in Perth, Gooch, without naming individuals, told one newspaper that the tour had been a nightmare and that he had been disappointed with the attitudes of certain players, who would not play for England while he was captain. I could not quarrel with his findings.

I felt at times that we didn't have sixteen people in Australia working towards one goal. I think in future before players are picked to go overseas the selectors should look beyond just their bowling and batting averages and ability and look at characters as well, since they have to be part of a team, living and travelling together for four and a half months. My definition of a good tourist is a bloke who is prepared 24 hours a day to do anything to better the side, whether it be bowling in the nets, getting lunch or a drink for a team-mate who may be exhausted in the middle of an innings, or training hard.

Those have always been the guidelines under which I have conducted myself. In Australia we had an abundance of ability, but when the chips were down there was not the 100 per cent togetherness that might have pulled us around from the experience of my previous tours.

12

LOOKING INTO THE
CRYSTAL BALL

There are many hard questions to answer as I face up to the future, not least of all nominating who will be bowling spin for England during the 1990s.

A decade earlier, in my first few years with Notts, the competition for an England place was fairly intense. Derek Underwood was still around though coming to the end of his career, and down at Middlesex John Emburey and Phil Edmonds were reaching their peaks. But the signs that we were not overendowed with a younger generation of players coming up behind them began to appear as early as the summer of 1984 when Pat Pocock suddenly reappeared on the England scene.

The Surrey off spinner had played fifteen Tests between 1967 and 1976, but had generally been overlooked for eight years when suddenly he was recalled after an eight-year absence from the England side for two Tests against the West Indies. He then went on to tour India the following winter under David Gower. Although both Vic Marks and myself had been given opportunities a couple of years earlier, it said much for the shortage of spinners around the county circuit that the selectors felt they had to turn back to Pocock at the age of 38.

While that situation may have seemed pretty desperate at the time, to my mind little has been done in the intervening years to put it right, which was probably why I went to Australia at the ripe old age of 41.

It's easy to fire arrows off in all directions, laying the blame for the dearth of spin bowlers, but quite impossible to be totally specific. I would say that the growth of the one-day game in England during the seventies has been as big a factor as any. In those days many county captains felt that because it was easier to slog slow bowling, medium pacers were generally the best weapon to use in the one-day game, bowling a tight line just short of a driving length outside the off stump.

To a certain extent it was not a bad policy from a tactical point of view, although people like Jack Simmonds, John Emburey and myself all proved at times to be an exception to the rule. Generally though it greatly retarded the development of many young spinners and probably kept several promising players out of the county game altogether. It was purely a case of economics – success in one-day games started to bring back big crowds to county grounds which had long since been deserted for Championship matches, and some county administrators could not see the point in spending several years grooming young players who would be of only limited use to their sides.

That was a big mistake which has now rebounded on English cricket; furthermore it was a fallacy, protecting youngsters from big hitters in limited-overs cricket. One of the main parts of spin bowling is control – an attribute only acquired through years of hard work and patience – and there can be no bigger test for a young spinner than trying to keep down the runs in a limited-overs game when the batsmen are looking to cut loose. Any young bowler who could succeed under such circumstances would have more than enough confidence to make the grade in the Championship.

Unfortunately the development of the five-man all-seam Sunday attack became the norm with county captains, and

135

that had another knock-on effect as those captains began to age and retire from the game. A new generation of county captains grew up, having learned nothing from their predecessors about the handling of spin bowling and the placement of fields that are so crucial to the art, so it's not only the bowlers, but also the captains with a belief in spin, that have disappeared from the game.

At Notts I have been lucky to escape that syndrome being fortunate for so many years to play under Clive Rice. When Mike Bore and I were bowling together for several seasons we had the full confidence of Rice, who at times would even chuck me the new ball straightaway if he thought it would win us a match. Watching Clive for all those years Tim Robinson, who later took his job, learned to appreciate his spinners which is why I fully expect to be working hard with Andy Afford over the next couple of summers.

Having outlined the history of the present situation, what will England do in future? It is my firm belief that the days are fast disappearing when it will be possible for a spinner to play Test cricket for this country, if all he can do is bowl and has nothing more to offer the side in the way of runs with the bat or sharp and alert fielding. Modern captains would view such a specialist as a waste of space.

It may well influence the future career of Phil Tufnell who at times looked a slow left arm bowler of great promise in Australia, but was shown to be lacking in the other two departments.

In the West Indies in early 1990 I had hopes for Keith Medlycott, who while not having Tufnell's control is a much bigger spinner of the ball and, as his record with Surrey shows, is quite capable of averaging 30 with the bat in a summer. Sadly after his return from the Caribbean Medlycott did not have the happiest of times back with Surrey and although later chosen to tour Sri Lanka with the A team there were widespread reports that he had lost both his action and confidence.

I would be accused of bias if I promoted my Notts colleague Afford for an England place, though certainly as a bowler he has plenty of potential. The problem is his weakness with the bat and in the field and I have often stressed to him that he must work on those facets of his game.

Given the limitations of the three mentioned above, only one other candidate immediately springs to mind and that is Worcestershire's Richard Illingworth, although he is a couple of years older. He is certainly not a big spinner, but he has good control, has scored a century in county cricket and is a top-class fielder close to the bat.

It hurts to admit that all those four are slow left-arm bowlers but there are even fewer off spinners around. A lot of hope is being held out for Robert Croft of Glamorgan, but barely out of his teens he still has much to learn, though he is already showing great promise with both bat and ball. I just hope for his and England's sake that his talent is carefully nurtured and that he is not pushed too far too quickly in the urge to find my immediate successor.

As I write in early March after returning from Australia, it is too early to predict what the selectors will do for the tough home series about to be played against the West Indies, which will be a daunting arena for any young spinner. I feel it is probable that the England attack will be based around pace and with Devon Malcolm and Angus Fraser available to lead the attack it is a justifiable policy.

But there will be times when England will need a spinner and that leaves another possible scenario. After seven years spent waiting in the wings Graeme Hick qualifies to play for England in the summer of 1991 and it has often been said that he will walk into the Test side. Doubts have been raised about his big match temperament since he failed in two Lord's finals with Worcestershire and struggled early on in the winter of 1990–91 when he signed to spend a season with Queensland in the highly competitive Sheffield Shield. I think, after so many successful seasons with Worcestershire, bowlers were beginning to find that if he had a weakness it was against high quality short-pitched bowling – anything less and he committed murder out in the middle.

However, should the selectors decide that Hick is the answer to their prayers, and that may well be known by the time this book is published, they will be picking a player who is capable of bowling off spin. Hick is not a frontline artist with the ball, but having worked hard over the years on that aspect of his game he is no mug either. With Mike Atherton trying too hard to develop his leg spin, in the immediate future I can foresee England going into Tests with a seam attack and using the two part-time bowlers in the event of spin being absolutely vital to the gameplan.

It is not a development that I would like to see, but when there are few if any viable alternatives, sadly it may well happen and English cricket will be the poorer for it.

It is all too easy to be critical of the current situation and it is only fair to offer constructive suggestions for the future. Efforts have got to be made all the way down the line to try to encourage spinners. It's too late to do anything now to solve the immediate crisis since spin bowlers cannot be produced out of a hat. But captains have got to be made more aware of their value in a balanced cricket team and counties have got to be patient with their development – a young lad taken on the staff must be given four to five years to develop and not just thrown out after a couple of seasons because he is not running through sides every day of the week. And youngsters must be given a chance to prove themselves in one-day competitions.

A lot has been said and written about the uncovering of pitches, but most of it is nonsense. While spinners always did thrive on the old sticky dogs so too did the medium pace seamers. What is needed are dry hard wickets with bounce which wear late on in the game and give spinners help in the last innings. Unfortunately in England for many years our pitches have started off with too much moisture in them and any which have turned too early have immediately been reported to Lord's as unsuitable.

There would of course be one other benefit from bringing spinners back into the English game – it would help our batsmen on winter tours overseas to places like India, Pakistan and Sri Lanka, where slow bowling is still considered a vital part of Test cricket and where our batsmen have often been bemused in the recent past.

I have often been asked whether I would like to stay in the game after retirement and help the development of the next generation of spinners, but it is not a job that could be done on a part-time or voluntary basis. It would take a lot of time and money to travel around the counties unearthing new talent and providing the necessary coaching over the several years it would take to develop spinners from scratch. While it should be a priority, given the current state of our game, and while there exists a generation of retired spinners with plenty of advice and experience to pass on, I doubt whether the people who hold the purse strings at Lord's would be willing to splash out on such a long-term project.

In fact I haven't thought too much about my own long-term future. Since returning from Australia I have grown to accept that my Test career is over and, while it is sad, at least I can say I have achieved my ambition of playing for my country and, for the most part, enjoyed every minute of it.

Although the selectors will be searching for a new generation of slow bowlers, I have no intention of quitting the game altogether just yet. I have two years of a contract with Notts still to run and I am looking forward not only to seeing that out but also to playing on afterwards if I can. Obviously that will depend largely on fitness, but since that is a side of the game that I have always worked hard on, I cannot see that posing a problem yet.

Ambitions? Yes, I have still got them. For one thing, if the selectors turned round out of the blue and asked me to play for England again, I would jump at the opportunity. I would love to get into the position where I could decide for myself when to retire from international cricket, but I do not think it will arise as the decision has already been taken for me. With Notts, however, there are still four domestic trophies up for grabs each season and I shall be trying my hardest to make sure we win some more before I call it a day. I certainly think we have a team capable of fighting for the honours.

Both my sons are now at senior school and playing cricket. Thomas is a seam bowler who bats a bit, while James is basically a batsman who bowls a bit. Before there is any talk of them following in their father's footsteps, I would like them to get a decent education first and I will not push them into cricket. If either of them is good enough and wants to play sport to earn a living then that would be great, but I will tell them first that it's not all glamour. It is a lot of hard work and there can be many disappointments, but for twenty-five years cricket has been my life and in general I can have no complaints.

CAREER STATISTICS

BATTING - In England

Year	Matches	Inns	NO	Runs	HS	Avge	100	50
1966	1	1	1	0	0*	-	-	-
1967	1	1	1	0	0*	-	-	-
1968	8	13	1	121	43	10.08	-	-
1969	12	20	7	281	45	21.61	-	-
1970	12	17	7	354	54	35.40	-	1
1971	22	30	3	641	80	23.74	-	3
1972	-	-	-	-	-	-	-	-
1973	16	26	4	530	54	24.09	-	1
1974	23	32	5	645	74	23.88	-	3
1975	21	36	10	587	69*	22.57	-	1
1976	24	32	11	444	76*	21.14	-	1
1977	23	30	5	413	85	16.52	-	1
1978	14	18	4	275	51	19.64	-	1
1979	21	31	6	453	85*	18.12	-	2
1980	24	28	4	496	86	20.66	-	1
1981	22	23	4	257	44	13.52	-	-
1982	20	25	8	432	127*	30.07	1	-
1983	23	32	3	377	38	13.00	-	-
1984	24	24	7	248	35	14.58	-	-
1985	21	22	5	297	56*	17.47	-	1
1986	21	23	4	330	54*	17.36	-	1
1987	25	27	8	389	75	20.47	-	3
1988	17	25	10	245	31*	16.33	-	-
1989	22	32	7	505	58*	20.20	-	2
1990	17	20	5	333	83	22.20	-	2

BATTING - Overseas

Year	M	Inns	NO	Runs	HS	Avge	100	50
1974-75	2	1	0	12	12	12.00	-	-
1981-82	3	6	1	51	20*	10.20	-	-
1982-83	6	10	3	228	95	32.57	-	2
1987-88	7	4	2	43	34	14.33	-	-
1989-90	4	6	1	13	6	2.60	-	-
1990-91	3	5	0	19	13	3.80	-	-

BOWLING - In England

Year	Overs	Mdns	Runs	Wkts	Avge	Best	5wI	10wM
1966	30.0	8	76	2	38.00	2-26	-	-
1967	17.0	4	61	3	20.33	2-25	-	-
1968	235.3	51	779	21	37.09	6-90	1	-
1969	194.2	37	566	18	31.44	4-40	-	-
1970	228.0	70	634	14	45.28	4-88	-	-
1971	419.4	108	1101	27	40.77	4-28	-	-
1972	-	-	-	-	-	-	-	-
1973	461.0	128	1208	38	31.78	5-43	1	-

1974	738.0	214	1855	84	22.08	7-57	6	1
1975	897.4	238	2456	79	31.08	7-33	4	1
1976	967.1	282	2488	81	30.71	7-92	5	2
1977	576.1	157	1690	46	36.73	6-82	2	1
1978	376.1	88	1142	28	40.87	4-51	-	-
1979	738.0	225	1770	62	28.54	5-74	2	-
1980	622.5	171	1700	77	22.07	7-62	4	-
1981	804.2	253	1857	90	20.63	7-59	6	2
1982	666.1	202	1611	64	25.17	6-76	3	-
1983	710.4	195	2000	59	33.89	7-23	2	1
1984	797.5	234	2220	94	23.61	7-47	7	2
1985	716.3	171	2103	55	38.23	6-51	2	-
1986	818.3	259	2134	73	29.23	7-102	5	2
1987	872.4	295	2119	88	24.14	6-62	7	1
1988	508.5	139	1312	42	31.23	4-50	-	-
1989	663.2	172	1720	58	29.65	6-87	2	-
1990	688.2	197	1844	51	36.15	6-58	2	-

BOWLING - Overseas

Year	Overs	Mdns	Runs	Wkts	Avge	Best	5wI	10wM
1974-75	41.0	7	141	4	35.25	3-32	-	-
1981-82	113.0	22	316	8	39.50	3-30	-	-
1982-83	372.3	98	964	33	29.21	10-175	2	1
1987-88	226.1	60	579	11	52.63	4-70	-	-
1989-90	108.1	30	301	15	20.06	5-77	1	-
1990-91	164.0	45	391	15	26.06	4-29	-	-

BEST PERFORMANCES IN FIRST-CLASS CRICKET

BATTING - In England

100s (1)

1982	127*	Nottinghamshire v Yorkshire	Worksop

50s (24)

1970	54	Warwickshire v Middlesex	Lord's
1971	63	Warwickshire v Surrey	Edgbaston
	80	Warwickshire v Worcestershire	Worcester
	55*	Warwickshire v Worcestershire	Edgbaston
1973	54	Warwickshire v Middlesex	Lord's
1974	56	Warwickshire v Glamorgan	Edgbaston
	50*	Warwickshire v Cambridge University	Nuneaton
	74	Warwickshire v Pakistanis	Edgbaston
1975	69*	Warwickshire v Hampshire	Edgbaston
1976	76*	Warwickshire v Surrey	Edgbaston
1977	85	Warwickshire v Essex	Edgbaston
1978	51	Warwickshire v Essex	Colchester
1979	73	Nottinghamshire v Cambridge University	Fenner's
	85*	Nottinghamshire v Hampshire	Bournemouth
1980	86	Nottinghamshire v Worcestershire	Worcester
1985	56*	Nottinghamshire v Glamorgan	Swansea
1886	54*	Nottinghamshire v Northamptonshire	Trent Bridge

142

1987	54	Nottinghamshire v Surrey	Trent Bridge
	66	Nottinghamshire v Lancashire	Old Trafford
	75	Nottinghamshire v Warwickshire	Worksop
1989	58*	Nottinghamshire v Yorkshire	Trent Bridge
	53	MCC v World XI	Scarborough
1990	83	Nottinghamshire v Leicestershire	Leicester
	51	England v India	The Oval

BATTING - Overseas

50s (2)

| 1982-83 | 60* | England XI v South Australia | Adelaide |
| | 95 | England v Australia (5th Test) | Sydney |

BOWLING - In England

Five or more wickets in an innings (61)

1968	6-90	Warwickshire v Hampshire	Edgbaston
1973	5-43	Warwickshire v Northamptonshire	Northampton
1974	5-91	Warwickshire v Worcestershire (1st inn)	Edgbaston
	7-76	Warwickshire v Worcestershire (2nd inn)	Edgbaston
	6-56	Warwickshire v Nottinghamshire	Trent Bridge
	7-57	Warwickshire v Lancashire	Edgbaston
	6-87	Warwickshire v Gloucestershire	Edgbaston
	6-45	Warwickshire v Lancashire	Old Trafford
1975	7-33	Warwickshire v Cambridge U (1st inn)	Fenner's
	5-31	Warwickshire v Cambridge U (2nd inn)	Fenner's
	5-56	Warwickshire v Northamptonshire	Northampton
	7-40	Warwickshire v Oxford University	The Parks
1976	6-43	Warwickshire v Kent	TunbridgeWells
	5-127	Warwickshire v Gloucestershire	Edgbaston
	6-145	Warwickshire v Hampshire (1st inn)	Bournemouth
	7-92	Warwickshire v Hampshire (2nd inn)	Bournemouth
	6-40	Warwickshire v Essex	Leyton
1977	6-82	Warwickshire v Somerset (1st inn)	Taunton
	5-83	Warwickshire v Somerset (2nd inn)	Taunton
1979	5-75	Nottinghamshire v Somerset	Weston-s-Mare
	5-74	Nottinghamshirev Warwickshire	Edgbaston
1980	7-62	Nottinghamshire v Leicestershire	Leicester
	5-67	Nottinghamshire v Yorkshire (1st inn)	Harrogate
	6-127	Nottinghamshire v Yorkshire (2nd inn)	Harrogate
	6-37	Nottinghamshire v Kent	Trent Bridge
1981	6-80	Nottinghamshire v Kent	Canterbury
	6-21	Nottinghamshire v Gloucestershire	Trent Bridge
	6-66	Nottinghamshire v Worcestershie	Worcester
	5-94	Nottinghamshire v Sussex	Trent Bridge
	7-59	Nottinghamshire v Derbyshire (1st inn)	Trent Bridge
	6-70	Nottinghamshire v Derbyshire (2nd inn)	Trent Bridge
1982	5-71	Nottinghamshire v Cambridge University	Fenner's
	5-31	Nottinghamshire v Gloucestershire	Cheltenham
	6-76	Nottinghamshire v Glamorgan	Swansea
1983	7-23	Nottinghamshire v Lancashire	Trent Bridge
	5-102	Nottinghamshire v Gloucestershire	Bristol

143

1984	6-50	Nottinghamshire v Glamorgan (1st inn)	Trent Bridge
	6-73	Nottinghamshire v Glamorgan (2nd inn)	Trent Bridge
	7-47	Nottinghamshire v Sri Lankans	Cleethorpes
	5-78	Nottinghamshire v Lancashire	Blackpool
	6-49	Nottinghamshire v Warwickshire	Trent Bridge
	6-93	Nottinghamshire v Northamptonshire	Trent Bridge
	5-111	Nottinghamshire v Sussex	Hove
1985	5-115	Nottinghamshire v Glamorgan	Trent Bridge
	6-51	Nottinghamshire v Lancashire	Trent Bridge
1986	7-102	Nottinghamshire v Essex	Chelmsford
	5-70	Nottinghamshire v Lancashire (1st inn)	Southport
	5-105	Nottinghamshire v Lancashire (2nd inn)	Southport
	5-107	Nottinghamshire v Derbyshire	Trent Bridge
	6-45	Nottinghamshire v Glamorgan	Cardiff
1987	6-99	Nottinghamshire v Surrey	Trent Bridge
	5-70	Nottinghamshire v Kent	Canterbury
	5-38	Nottinghamshire v Derbyshire	Derby
	6-62	Nottinghamshire v Warwickshire	Worksop
	5-19	Nottinghamshire v Northamptonshire	Trent Bridge
	5-112	Nottinghamshire v Essex	Chelmsford
	5-12	Nottinghamshire v Glamorgan	Trent Bridge
1989	6-87	Nottinghamshire v Surrey	Guildford
	5-20	Nottinghamshire v Derbyshire	Trent Bridge
1990	6-58	England v New Zealand	Edgbaston
	5-99	Nottinghamshire v Essex	Southend

Ten or more wickets in a match (13)

1974	12-167	Warwickshire v Worcestershire	Edgbaston
1975	12-64	Warwickshire v Cambridge University	Fenner's
1976	10-101	Warwickshire v Kent	Tunbridge Wells
	13-237	Warwickshire v Hampshire	Bournemouth
1977	11-165	Warwickshire v Somerset	Taunton
1980	11-194	Nottinghamshire v Yorkshire	Harrogate
1981	10-130	Nottinghamshire v Worcestershire	Worcester
	13-129	Nottinghamshire v Derbyshire	Trent Bridge
1983	11-77	Nottinghamshire v Lancashire	Trent Bridge
1984	12-123	Nottinghamshire v Glamorgan	Trent Bridge
1986	10-164	Nottinghamshire v Essex	Chelmsford
	10-175	Nottinghamshire v Lancashire	Southport
1987	10-79	Nottinghamshire v Warwickshire	Worksop

Hat-tricks

1977		Warwickshire v Worcestershire	Edgbaston
1984		Nottinghamshire v Northamptonshire	Northampton

BOWLING - Overseas

Five or more wickets in an innings (3)

1982-83	10-175	International XI v West Indian XI	Kingston
	5-101	England XI v New South Wales	Sydney
1989-90	5-77	England XI v Barbados	Bridgetown

144

Ten or more wickets in a match (1)

1982-83   10-175   International XI v West Indian XI   Kingston

TEST CAREER RECORD - MATCH BY MATCH

Year	Test	Opposition	Venue	Batting		Bowling		Ct
1982	1	Pakistan	Edgbaston	2	19	2-56	1-27	2
1982	2	Pakistan	Lord's	6	14	0-53	0-13	
1982-83	3	Australia	Brisbane	15*	18	0-81	2-43	1
1982-83	4	Australia	Adelaide	0	0	1-96	0-5	1
1982-83	5	Australia	Sydney	29	95	3-68	3-116	
1987-88	6	Pakistan	Faisalabad	1*		1-35	0-16	
1987-88	7	Australia	Sydney	8*		3-53	0-107	
1987-88	8	New Zealand	Wellington			0-107		
1989	9	Australia	Trent Bridge	38	35	0-81		
1990	10	New Zealand	Trent Bridge	13*		1-47	0-0	
1990	11	New Zealand	Lord's	0		2-67		
1990	12	New Zealand	Edgbaston	20	0	6-58	1-43	
1990	13	India	Lord's			2-109	2-79	
1990	14	India	Old Trafford	19		2-74	3-75	
1990	15	India	The Oval	51		2-117		
1990-91	16	Australia	Sydney	0		3-105	3-94	1

TEST CAREER RECORD - SERIES BY SERIES

BATTING and FIELDING

Year	Opposition	Tests	Inns	NO	Runs	HS	Avge	100	50	Ct
1982	Pakistan	2	4	0	41	19	10.25	-	-	2
1982-83	Australia	3	6	1	157	95	31.40	-	1	2
1987-88	Pakistan	1	1	1	1	1*	-	-	-	-
1987-88	Australia	1	1	1	8	8*	-	-	-	-
1987-88	New Zealand	1	-	-	-	-	-	-	-	-
1989	Australia	1	2	0	73	38	36.50	-	-	-
1990	New Zealand	3	4	1	33	20	11.00	-	-	-
1990	India	3	2	0	70	51	35.00	-	1	-
1990-91	Australia	1	1	0	0	0	0.00	-	-	1

BOWLING

Year	Opposition	Overs	Mdns	Runs	Wkts	Avge	Best	5wI	10wM
1982	Pakistan	56.1	12	149	3	49.66	2-56	-	-
1982-83	Australia	188.3	59	409	9	45.44	3-68	-	-
1987-88	Pakistan	25.0	8	51	1	51.00	1-35	-	-
1987-88	Australia	74.0	18	160	3	53.33	3-53	-	-
1987-88	New Zealand	45.0	15	107	0	-	-	-	-
1989	Australia	33.0	9	81	0	-	-	-	-
1990	New Zealand	107.3	44	215	10	21.50	6-58	1	-
1990	India	137.2	26	454	11	41.27	3-75	-	-
1990-91	Australia	73.0	16	199	6	33.16	3-94	-	-

BATTING and FIELDING

Opposition	Tests	Inns	NO	Runs	HS	Avge	100	50	Ct
Australia	6	10	2	238	95	29.75	-	1	3
New Zealand	4	4	1	33	20	11.00	-	-	-
India	3	2	0	70	51	35.00	-	1	-
Pakistan	3	5	1	42	19	10.50	-	-	2
Totals	16	21	4	383	95	22.52	-	2	5

BOWLING

Opposition	Overs	Mdns	Runs	Wkts	Avge	Best	5wI	10wM
Australia	368.3	102	849	18	47.72	3-53	-	-
New Zealand	152.3	59	322	10	32.20	6-58	1	-
India	137.2	26	454	11	41.27	3-75	-	-
Pakistan	81.1	20	200	4	50.00	2-56	-	-
Totals	739.3	207	1825	43	42.44	6-58	1	-

ONE-DAY INTERNATIONAL CAREER - MATCH BY MATCH

Year	Match	Opposition	Venue	Batting	Bowling	Ct
1982	1	Pakistan (PT)	Trent Bridge		0-45	1
1982	2	Pakistan (PT)	Old Trafford	1	1-30	
1982-83	3	Australia (WSC)	Sydney	3	3-11	
1982-83	4	New Zealand (WSC)	Adelaide		0-49	
1982-83	5	Australia (WSC)	Adelaide		1-40	
1987-88	6	Sri Lanka (WC)	Peshawar		2-31	1
1987-88	7	Pakistan (WC)	Karachi	4*	0-40	
1987-88	8	West Indies (WC)	Jaipur		2-46	1
1987-88	9	Sri Lanka (WC)	Pune		3-57	
1987-88	10	India (WC semi-final)	Bombay		4-52	
1987-88	11	Australia (WC final)	Calcutta		2-48	
1987-88	12	Pakistan	Lahore		2-44	
1987-88	13	Pakistan	Karachi		0-45	
1989-90	14	Sri Lanka (NC)	Delhi		1-34	
1989-90	15	Australia (NC)	Hyderabad		0-17	
1989-90	16	Pakistan (NC)	Cuttack		1-13	
1989-90	17	India (NC)	Kanpur		1-51	
1989-90	18	West Indies (NC)	Gwalior	1*	0-44	1
1989-90	19	West Indies	Port of Spain		1-41	
1989-90	20	West Indies	Port of Spain			
1989-90	21	West Indies	Kingston		3-31	
1989-90	22	West Indies	Georgetown	0*	1-33	
1989-90	23	West Indies	Georgetown	3*	1-37	
1989-90	24	West Indies	Bridgetown		1-32	
1990	25	New Zealand (TT)	Headingley		0-51	
1990	26	New Zealand (TT)	The Oval		0-34	
1990	27	India(TT)	Headingley	3	0-36	
1990	28	India (TT)	Trent Bridge	0	2-53	
1990-91	29	New Zealand (WSC)	Adelaide	3	1-51	
1990-91	30	New Zealand (WSC)	Sydney	8*	2-34	1
1990-91	31	Australia (WSC)	Brisbane	3*	0-57	
1990-91	32	Australia (WSC)	Sydney	1	1-57	
1990-91	33	New Zealand	Christchurch		1-50	

ONE-DAY INTERNATIONAL CAREER - SERIES BY SERIES

BATTING and FIELDING

Year	Competition	M	Inns	NO	Runs	HS	Avge	100	50	Ct
1982	v Pakistan	2	1	0	1	1	1.00	-	-	1
1982-83	World Series Cup	3	1	0	3	3	3.00	-	-	-
1987-88	World Cup	6	1	1	4	4*	-	-	-	2
1987-88	v Pakistan	2	-	-	-	-	-	-	-	-
1989-90	Nehru Cup	5	1	1	1	1*	-	-	-	1
1989-90	v West Indies	6	2	2	3	3*	-	-	-	-
1990	v New Zealand	2	-	-	-	-	-	-	-	-
1990	v India	2	2	0	3	3	1.50	-	-	-
1990-91	World Series Cup	4	4	2	15	8*	7.50	-	-	1
1990-91	v New Zealand	1	-	-	-	-	-	-	-	-

BOWLING

Year	Competition	Overs	Mdns	Runs	Wkts	Avge	Best	5wI
1982	v Pakistan	22.0	4	75	1	75.00	1-30	-
1982-83	World Series Cup	19.3	0	100	4	25.00	3-11	-
1987-88	World Cup	59.3	4	274	13	21.07	4-52	-
1987-88	v Pakistan	18.0	1	89	2	44.50	2-44	-
1989-90	Nehru Cup	33.0	1	159	3	53.00	1-13	-
1989-90	v West Indies	48.0	2	174	7	24.85	3-31	-
1990	v New Zealand	22.0	2	85	0	-	-	-
1990	v India	22.0	1	89	2	44.50	2-53	-
1990-91	World Series Cup	38.0	1	199	4	49.75	2-34	-
1990-91	v New Zealand	10.0	0	50	1	50.00	1-50	-

ONE-DAY INTERNATIONAL CAREER RECORD - AGAINST EACH OPPOSITION

BATTING and FIELDING

Opposition	M	Inns	NO	Runs	HS	Avge	100	50	Ct
Australia	6	3	1	7	3*	-	-	-	-
West Indies	8	3	3	4	3*	-	-	-	2
New Zealand	6	2	1	11	8*	11.00	-	-	1
India	4	2	0	3	3	1.50	-	-	-
Pakistan	6	2	1	5	4*	5.00	-	-	1
Sri Lanka	3	-	-	-	-	-	-	-	1
Totals	33	12	6	30	8*	5.00	-	-	5

BOWLING

Opposition	Overs	Mdns	Runs	Wkts	Avge	Best	5wI
Australia	45.3	1	230	7	32.85	3-11	-
West Indies	65.0	2	264	9	29.33	3-31	-
New Zealand	56.0	3	269	4	67.25	2-34	-
India	41.3	2	192	7	27.42	4-52	-
Pakistan	54.0	6	217	4	54.25	2-44	-
Sri Lanka	30.0	2	122	6	20.33	3-57	-
Totals	302.0	16	1293	37	34.94	4-52	-

BATTING and FIELDING

	Matches	Inns	NO	Runs	HS	Avge	100	50	Ct
Tests	16	21	4	383	95	22.52	-	2	5
All First-Class	459	600	137	9022	127*	19.37	1	26	190
One-Day Internationals	33	12	6	30	8*	5.00	-	-	5
Gillette / NatWest	39	28	9	233	31*	12.26	-	-	8
John Player / Refuge	253	165	51	1606	44*	14.08	-	-	75
Benson & Hedges	81	50	16	487	61*	14.32	-	1	19

BOWLING

	Balls	Runs	Wkts	Avge	Best	5wI	10wM
Tests	4437	1825	43	42.44	6-58	1	-
All First-Class	88599	39138	1340	29.20	10-175	64	14
One-Day Internationals	1752	1293	37	34.94	4-52	-	
Gillette / NatWest	2596	1456	44	33.09	3-27	-	
John Player / Refuge	9756	7498	259	28.95	5-22	4	
Benson & Hedges	4819	2515	72	34.93	4-47	-	

BEST PERFORMANCES

Tests	95	England v Australia	Sydney	1982-83
	6-58	England v New Zealand	Edgbaston	1990
First-class	127*	Nottinghamshire v Yorkshire	Worksop	1982
	10-175	International XI v West Indian XI	Kingston	1982-83

CAREER SUMMARY

Born: Leamington Spa, 20 February 1949
Debut for Warwickshire in 1966
Debut for Nottinghamshire in 1979
Test debut v Pakistan at Edgbaston in 1982
Overseas tours: D.H.Robins XI to South Africa (1974-75); International XI to Pakistan (1981-82); International XI to West Indies (1982-83); England to Australia and New Zealand (1982-83); England to India, Pakistan, New Zealand and Australia (1987-88); England to India and West Indies (1989-90); England to Australia and New Zealand (1990-91)